CAMBRIDGE GREEK TESTAMENT COMMENTARY

GENERAL EDITOR

C. F. D. MOULE

*Lady Margaret's Professor of Divinity in the
University of Cambridge*

THE EPISTLES OF
PAUL THE APOSTLE TO THE
COLOSSIANS AND TO
PHILEMON

THE EPISTLES OF PAUL THE APOSTLE TO THE COLOSSIANS AND TO PHILEMON

AN INTRODUCTION AND
COMMENTARY BY

C. F. D. MOULE

Fellow of Clare College
Lady Margaret's Professor of Divinity in the
University of Cambridge

CAMBRIDGE
AT THE UNIVERSITY PRESS
1968

Published by the Syndics of the Cambridge University Press
Bentley House, 200 Euston Road, London, N.W. 1
American Branch: 32 East 57th Street, New York, N.Y. 10022

Standard Book Number:
521 04252 6   Clothbound
521 09236 1   Paperback

First printed 1957
Reprinted 1958 1962 1968

Printed in Great Britain
at the University Printing House, Cambridge
(Brooke Crutchley, University Printer)

PREFACE

BY THE GENERAL EDITOR

The last fifty years have seen a considerable shift in emphasis within New Testament scholarship. When the primary task was to establish the text and to discuss the authenticity of the documents, linguistic and historical considerations were foremost. But gradually, as these foundation-tasks were done, it became possible to devote increasing attention to the elucidation of the theological and religious contents of the New Testament, and to see it in the setting of the life and worship of Christian communities.

To be sure, no scholarship worthy of the name had at any time neglected this aspect of New Testament studies; still less can this aspect be examined without the linguistic and historical: that would be to build on sand. Nor can the primary tasks ever be taken as completed once and for all. Foundations need continual re-examination and reinforcement.

Nevertheless, it is for the sake of the superstructure that foundations exist: and it is the superstructure which now rightly claims its due attention. Accordingly, the time seems ripe for a revision of the New Testament volumes of a long-established series of Cambridge biblical commentaries.

Not that the intention is—as yet, at any rate—to replace all the old volumes; still less to belittle those which are selected for replacement. It would be folly to despise a series begun under the editorship of J. J. S. Perowne with a galaxy of eminent collaborators, and maintained at a high standard ever since.

But it is believed that the new series, in a more attractive format and written with contemporary trends in view and with the advantage of such new material as has come to light, will meet a need.

The series began, in 1877, with *The Cambridge Bible for Schools* (on the English text) and, shortly afterwards, with *The Cambridge Greek Testament for Schools and Colleges*. At the present time, however, it seems better not to use titles suggesting any definition of the readers. There are many beyond school age who will welcome a commentary without Greek; and there are some outside the Universities who will use one on the Greek text. The new series—confining itself for the time being to the Greek Testament—will therefore be called simply the *Cambridge Greek Testament Commentary*.

The first General Editor of this new series was Professor A. M. Ramsey; and it was under him that the first contributors, including the present General Editor, were enrolled. Professor Ramsey's elevation to the See of Durham, however, led to his resignation; and at about the same time one of the pledged collaborators, the Rev. R. G. Heard, Dean of Peterhouse, was removed by death.

It falls to the new General Editor to take up the midwifery, and this he is proud to attempt—although, like his predecessors, he does not accept responsibility for all the views expressed by the children, but only for their general character and conduct.

et sit splendor Domini Dei nostri super nos!
et opus manuum nostrarum dirige.

Amen.

C.F.D.M.

CAMBRIDGE
1955

CONTENTS

Preface by the General Editor   *page* v

List of Abbreviations   ix

INTRODUCTION

I. THE RELIGIOUS THOUGHT OF THE EPISTLES
   TO THE COLOSSIANS AND TO PHILEMON   3
   1. Christ   3
   2. The Church   6
   3. Becoming a Christian   8
   4. Prayer   10
   5. Ethics   10

II. THE CIRCUMSTANCES WHICH LED TO THE
    WRITING OF THE EPISTLES TO THE COLOS-
    SIANS AND TO PHILEMON   13
    1. Authorship   13
    2. Goodspeed and Knox on Philemon   14
    3. Alternative views   18
    4. Where was St Paul?   21
    5. St Paul's friends   25
    6. The situation addressed   29

III. TEXTUAL CRITICISM OF THE PAULINE
     EPISTLES   37
     1. Materials   38
     2. Principles   40

CONTENTS

NOTES

THE EPISTLE TO THE COLOSSIANS   *page* 45

THE EPISTLE TO PHILEMON   140

APPENDIX OF DISCURSIVE NOTES

I. A NOTE ON CHRISTIAN GREETINGS IN
     LETTERS   153

II. A NOTE ON ἀπόστολος   155

III. A NOTE ON THE KNOWLEDGE OF GOD   159

IV. A NOTE ON πλήρωμα   164

V. A NOTE ON THE REFLEXIVE PRONOUN   169

LIST OF ABBREVIATIONS

Books or articles cited more than once are (with rare exceptions) described by abbreviated titles; commentaries on Colossians are cited by the name of the author alone. The details are given below. Otherwise, the details are, in most cases, given at the citation.

COMMENTARIES

ABBOTT, T. K., *The Epistles to the Ephesians and to the Colossians* (*The International Critical Commentary*, Edinburgh, n.d.).

BIEDER, W., *Brief an die Kolosser* (in *Prophezei* series, Zürich, 1943).

DIBELIUS, M., *An die Kolosser, Epheser, an Philemon* (Lietzmann's *Handbuch zum Neuen Testament*, Tübingen, 3rd ed. revised by H. Greeven, 1953).

DODD, C. H., *Colossians* and *Philemon* in *The Abingdon Commentary* (Epworth Press, 1929).

LIGHTFOOT, J. B., *St Paul's Epistles to the Colossians and to Philemon* (London, 2nd ed., 1876).

LOHMEYER, E., *Die Briefe an die Philipper, Kolosser und an Philemon* (Meyer's *Kritisch-exegetischer Kommentar über das Neue Testament*, Göttingen, 9th ed. edited by W. Schmauch, 1953).

MASSON, C., *L'Épître de Saint Paul aux Colossiens* (*Commentaire du Nouveau Testament*, x, P. Bonnard, *L'Épître de Saint Paul aux Philippiens* and C. Masson, *ut sup.*, Neuchatel and Paris, 1950).

PEAKE, A. S., *The Epistle of Paul to the Colossians* (in *The Expositor's Greek Testament*, vol. III, London, 1903).

RADFORD, L. B., *The Epistle to the Colossians and the Epistle to Philemon* (*The Westminister Commentary*, London, 1931).

RENDTORFF, H., *Das Neue Testament Deutsch*, 8. *Die Kleineren Briefe des Apostels Paulus* (Göttingen, 1949).

VINCENT, M. R., *The Epistles to the Philippians and to Philemon* (*The International Critical Commentary*, Edinburgh, 1897).

WILLIAMS, A. LUKYN, *The Epistles of Paul the Apostle to the Colossians and to Philemon* (*The Cambridge Greek Testament for Schools and Colleges*, Cambridge, 1907).

OTHER BOOKS AND ARTICLES

ABEL: F.-M. ABEL, *Grammaire du grec biblique suivie d'un choix de papyrus* (Paris, 1927).

BAUER: W. BAUER, *Griechisch-Deutsches Wörterbuch zu den Schriften des Neuen Testaments und der übrigen urchristlichen Literatur* (Berlin, 4th ed. 1952).

BEST, *One Body*: E. BEST, *One Body in Christ* (S.P.C.K., 1955).

BONSIRVEN, *Paul*: J. BONSIRVEN, *L'Évangile de Paul* (Paris, 1948).

BORNKAMM, *Ende*: G. BORNKAMM, *Das Ende des Gesetzes* (Munich, 1952).

BURTON, *Galatians*: E. DE W. BURTON, *The Epistle to the Galatians* (*The International Critical Commentary*, Edinburgh, 1921).

CULLMANN, *C.T.*: O. CULLMANN, *Christ and Time* (London, 1951, translated by F. V. Filson from *Christus und die Zeit*).

DAVIES, *Paul*: W. D. DAVIES, *Paul and Rabbinic Judaism* (S.P.C.K., 1948).

D.-B.: A. DEBRUNNER, Friedrich Blass, *Grammatik des neutestamentlichen Griechisch*, bearbeitet von A. Debrunner (Göttingen, 7th ed. 1943).

DODD, *F.G.*: C. H. DODD, *The Interpretation of the Fourth Gospel* (Cambridge, 1953).

DUPONT-SOMMER: A. DUPONT-SOMMER, *The Jewish Sect of Qumran and the Essenes* (London, 1954), translated by R. D. Barnett from *Nouveaux Aperçus sur les manuscrits de la mer Morte* (Paris, 1953).

FIELD, *Otium*: F. FIELD, *Otium Norvicense* (three parts, Oxford, 1881).

GEORGE, *Communion*: A. R. GEORGE, *Communion with God* (Epworth Press, 1953).

GOODENOUGH, 'P. and O'.: E. R. GOODENOUGH, 'Paul and Onesimus' (in *Harvard Theological Review*, XXII, 1929, pp. 181 ff.).

GOODSPEED, *Meaning of Eph.*: E. J. GOODSPEED, *The Meaning of Ephesians* (Chicago, 1933).

GOODSPEED, *New Solutions*: E. J. GOODSPEED, *New Solutions of New Testament Problems* (Chicago, 1927).

HARRISON, 'O. and P.': P. N. HARRISON, 'Onesimus and Philemon' in *The Anglican Theological Review*, vol. XXXII (Oct. 1950), pp. 268–94.

J. Knox, *Marcion*: John Knox, *Marcion and the New Testament* (Chicago, 1942).

J. Knox, *Philemon*: John Knox, *Philemon among the Letters of Paul* (Chicago, 1935).

W. L. Knox, *Gentiles*: W. L. Knox, *St Paul and the Church of the Gentiles* (Cambridge, 1939).

W. L. Knox, *Jerusalem*: W. L. Knox, *St Paul and the Church of Jerusalem* (Cambridge, 1925).

L. & S.: H. G. Liddell & R. Scott, *A Greek-English Lexicon*, new edition, revised and augmented throughout by H. Stuart Jones (Oxford, 1925–40).

Manson, *The Church's Ministry*: T. W. Manson, *The Church's Ministry* (London, 1948).

Masson, *Eph.*: C. Masson, *L'Épître de Saint Paul aux Éphésiens* (*Commentaire du Nouveau Testament*, ix, P. Bonnard, *L'Épître de Saint Paul aux Galates* and C. Masson, *ut sup.*, Neuchatel and Paris, 1953).

Mersch, *The Whole Christ*: E. Mersch, *The Whole Christ* (English trans. by J. R. Kelley, London, 1949).

Mitton, *Eph.*: C. L. Mitton, *The Epistle to the Ephesians* (Oxford, 1951).

M.M.: J. H. Moulton and G. Milligan, *The Vocabulary of the Greek Testament* (London, 1930).

Moffatt, *I.L.N.T.*: J. Moffatt, *An Introduction to the Literature of the New Testament* (Edinburgh, 2nd ed. 1912).

Percy, *Probleme*: E. Percy, *Die Probleme der Kolosser- und Epheserbriefe* (Lund, 1946).

Preiss, *Life in Christ*: Théo Preiss, 'Vie en Christ et éthique sociale dans L'Épître à Philémon' in *Aux Sources de la Tradition Chrétienne* (Goguel Festschrift, 1950). English trans. by H. Knight in *Life in Christ* (S.C.M., 1952), ch. II.

Robinson, *Eph.*: J. A. Robinson, *St Paul's Epistle to the Ephesians* (London, 1903).

Robinson, *The Body*: J. A. T. Robinson, *The Body* (S.C.M., 1952).

Roller, *Formular*: O. Roller, *Das Formular der paulinischen Briefe* (Stuttgart, 1933).

S.-B.: H. L. Strack and P. Billerbeck, *Kommentar zum Neuen Testament aus Talmud und Midrasch* (Munich, 1922–8).

SCHUBERT, 'Form and Function': P. SCHUBERT, 'The Form and Function of the Pauline Thanksgivings' (*Z.N.T.W.*, Beiheft 20, 1939).

SCHWEITZER, *Mysticism*: A. SCHWEITZER, *The Mysticism of Paul the Apostle* (London, 1931; trans. by W. Montgomery of *Die Mystik des Apostels Paulus*, 1930).

SCOTT, *St Paul*: C. A. A. SCOTT, *Christianity according to St Paul* (Cambridge, 1932).

SEIDENSTICKER, *Opfer*: P. SEIDENSTICKER, *Lebendiges Opfer* (Münster, 1954).

SELWYN, *I Peter*: E. G. SELWYN, *The First Epistle of St Peter* (London, 1946).

Studia Paulina: J. N. SEVENSTER and W. C. VAN UNNIK (edd.), *Studia Paulina in honorem J. de Zwaan* (Haarlem, 1953).

V. TAYLOR, *Names*: V. TAYLOR, *The Names of Jesus* (London, 1953).

THORNTON, *Common Life*: L. S. THORNTON, *The Common Life in the Body of Christ* (Dacre Press, n.d., introduction dated 1941).

T.W.N.T.: G. KITTEL (ed.), continued by G. FRIEDRICH (ed.), *Theologisches Wörterbuch zum Neuen Testament* (Stuttgart, 1933–).

VAN UNNIK, *Verlossing*: W. C. VAN UNNIK, *De Verlossing I Petrus i. 18–19* (Amsterdam, 1942).

WETTSTEIN: J. J. WETTSTEIN, *Novum Testamentum* (Amsterdam, 1751).

WINDISCH, *Weisheit*: H. WINDISCH, *Die göttliche Weisheit der Juden und die paulinische Christologie* (Leipzig, 1914).

JOURNALS

A.J.T.: *American Journal of Theology*, Chicago.

B.J.R.L.: *Bulletin of the John Rylands Library at Manchester*.

E.T.: *The Expository Times*, Edinburgh.

H.T.R.: *Harvard Theological Review*, Cambridge, Mass. (earlier issues, New York).

J.B.L.: *Journal of Biblical Literature*, Philadelphia, Pa. (earlier issues, Boston).

J.N.T.S.: *Journal of New Testament Studies*, Cambridge.

J.T.S.: *Journal of Theological Studies*, Oxford.

S.J.T.: *Scottish Journal of Theology*, Edinburgh.

Z.N.T.W.: *Zeitschrift für die neutestamentliche Wissenschaft*, Giessen.

Z.T.K.: *Zeitschrift für Theologie und Kirche*, Freiburg i. B.

TEXTS

W.H.: B. F. WESTCOTT and F. J. A. HORT, *The New Testament in Greek* (*editio maior*, 2 vols., Cambridge and Macmillan, 1881; *editio minor*, one vol. without introduction, etc., 1895).

The commentary is based on the British and Foreign Bible Society's text (second edition, of which the proofs were made available by the courtesy of Professor G. D. Kilpatrick), and the *sigla* of the apparatus of that edition (referred to as 'the Bible Society') are mainly used. Thus D etc. in the textual notes = D_2 etc. alluded to on pp. 38f. LXX = The 'Septuagint' Greek version of the Old Testament.

PATRISTIC AND OTHER QUOTATIONS

Theod. Mops.: Theodore of Mopsuestia, in the annotated edition of H. B. SWETE (2 vols., Cambridge, 1880).

Other citations from the Greek and Latin Fathers are chiefly from their commentaries on the passages in question; otherwise the edition and reference are usually indicated at the citation.

The citations from Philo are from L. COHN's edition (Berlin, 1896); and those from Classical writers follow the standard editions.

NOTE

Certain important books had not become readily accessible before the MS. went to press. Of especial value as a balanced and readable account of the 'Dead Sea Scrolls' (see p. 32) is M. BURROWS, *The Dead Sea Scrolls* (New York, 1955); and, for E. J. GOODSPEED's views (see p. 14), add, now, his *The Key to Ephesians* (Chicago, 1956).

INTRODUCTION

I. THE RELIGIOUS THOUGHT OF
THE EPISTLES TO THE COLOSSIANS
AND TO PHILEMON

1. CHRIST

If one were compelled to select the single most striking aspect of the letter to the Christians at Colossae, the choice would probably fall upon its description, in verses few but almost intolerably weighty, of *Christ* and of *his position in relation to the universe and the Church*. For insight into other famous aspects of what this most vivid of evangelists preached (reasons will be advanced later for holding Colossians to be genuinely Pauline), one might turn first to other letters—to Galatians and Romans for deliverance from a legalistic religion, to the Thessalonian letters for certain conceptions of the Final Act of God's purpose (which in Colossians is not prominent: see on iii. 1–4), to the Corinthian letters for a variety of matters concerning community life and Christian doctrine. All these letters contain also very notable references to the position of Jesus in Christian faith. But nowhere is more striking evidence to be found of the way in which the 'Nazarene impostor' had taken up his position as Lord than in Colossians, which (assuming its Pauline authorship) may be dated at latest some thirty to thirty-five years after that Nazarene's ignominious death.

The 'Great Christology' of Col. i. 15 ff. is discussed in the notes on the text, where evidence is given for the origin of some of the words and phrases in Jewish and possibly pagan religious writings. But its most striking aspect is concerned with the origins not of the vocabulary, but of the conviction which led to Jesus of Nazareth being described

3

with such a wealth of divine attributes. How was it that the crucified Nazarene came to occupy such a position in the faith of Christians? The main answer, no doubt, lies in the resurrection. It was this which had designated him Son of God (Rom. i. 4) and had brought to his followers the assurance that his was the ultimate triumph which now only waited to be revealed. And when they reflected on this, they were doubtless led to cast their minds not only forward to his future manifestation in glory, but backwards also to his pre-existent glory. If Jesus was enthroned as King of the future, must he not also be equated with the Wisdom and Word of God who had been God's agent in creation, before the beginning of time? The resurrection carried implications in both directions. Moreover, it may be that the conviction that Christ was the new 'Torah'—God's new 'Law', or self-revelation—led in the same direction, since Torah was closely associated with the creative Wisdom of God.[1]

Not because he [Paul] is so filled with admiration for the pure ethics and the lofty religious teaching of the Sermon on the Mount [wrote B. W. Bacon]...still less because of acquaintance with, or dependence on particular writings such as the Wisdom of Solomon, and the philosophical mysticism of Philo...but because to an educated Hellenistic[2] Jew such as Paul, converted by such an experience as his to belief in Jesus as the exalted Servant, the leader of Israel in its God-given calling to bring the world into reconciliation with God, it was inevitable that he should think of him as the agent of God in creation, revelation and redemption.[3]

Another consideration was, even more practically and less speculatively, that Christian experience had come to find in Jesus a unique and satisfying way of forgiveness and of approach to God, with the result that all other ways of

[1] Davies, *Paul*, pp. 147 ff.
[2] Though it is a question how far such a description fits St Paul. See W. C. van Unnik, *Tarsus of Jeruzalem* (Amsterdam, 1952).
[3] *Jesus and Paul* (1921), pp. 132 f.

communication, known or imagined, became identified with him and included in him: in him were all the divine treasures (ii. 3). All this, be it noted, was seen by the Christians to be entirely in keeping with what the Jesus of history had been. Their present conviction was not a reversal of his ministry: it was part and parcel of it—its explanation and its consequence.

In the case of St Paul himself there was a further circumstance which may have contributed to this conviction, namely his encounter on the Damascus road with the risen Christ. It is far from unlikely that this blinding flash of revelation gave to the Apostle a peculiar unity of understanding. In it he came face to face with the renegade Nazarene, who had been duly executed and whose followers St Paul was persecuting, but who now showed himself as overwhelmingly alive and as identifying himself with his suffering Church ('...why persecutest thou *me*?' Acts ix. 4f., xxii. 7f., xxvi. 14f.), yet supreme over it and supernaturally splendid. Thus, at one stroke, the material and the spiritual, the past and the present, the Jesus of history and the Christ of faith were presented to him, in such a way that his descriptions of Christ include as a unity the various aspects which, for many other Christians, may have been only gradually taking up their positions as parts of a single whole. After such an experience, it was not merely conceivable that Jesus might be designated in terms of God's pre-cosmic activity: it was impossible to find terms sufficiently big to do justice to his fulness and inclusiveness. And, at the same time, there was never a shadow of doubt but that this majestic figure was identical with the Jesus of history—not a superimposed idea, but the same person. St Paul's conception of Christ is not derived from a Jewish conception of Messiah, but from the actual Jesus.[1]

Even so, it may have taken St Paul some time to reach so

[1] Cf. F. C. Porter, *The Mind of Christ in Paul* (Scribner's, 1932), p. 25.

articulate an expression of these convictions as is found in Colossians; and the errors current at Colossae may well themselves have acted as a further stimulus to his formulation of them.[1] Of that, more will be said later.

2. THE CHURCH

Meanwhile, what else is there of peculiar moment doctrinally in this epistle? It is in no sense a complete exposition of Christian beliefs, and does not purport to be. It contains, for instance, practically nothing about the Spirit (see on i. 8), or about faith. But there is in it much food for thought about *the nature and function of the Christian Church,* and, in particular, there is the profound conception of the Church as the Body of Christ. The notes on i. 18 call attention to the fact that Christ appears as the Head of the Body here and in Ephesians, but not in the earlier epistles, where he is the Body, simply. But it is not clear that this distinction is particularly important.[2] What is important, in either case, is the daring conception of Christians as the Body of Christ or as his limbs. Whatever may have been the pre-Christian uses of the words 'body' and 'limbs' as metaphors for a collective whole with integrated parts, here is something new and different: Christians are not 'the body of Christians', nor merely limbs of one another (though they are that), but the body and limbs of Christ.[3] It may have been St Paul's experience of the risen Christ as identified with his persecuted followers (so in all three accounts in the

[1] It is worth while to consider whether T. W. Manson's suggestion (*B.J.R.L.* xxxii, 1 (Sept. 1949)) that Hebrews may have been written by Apollos *to Colossae* throws light on the situation. Is Heb. i. 2, κληρονόμον πάντων, parallel to the πλήρωμα idea of Colossians? In *E.T.* lxii, 10 (July 1951), R. L. Archer suggests that Apollos was the source of St Paul's (virtual) Logos-doctrine.

[2] Cullmann, *C.T.*, p. 187, remarks that Christ is Head both of the universe and of the Church, but that only the Church is his Body. See also Best, *One Body*, p. 123.

[3] T. W. Manson, *J.T.S.* xxxvii, no. 148 (Oct. 1936), p. 385.

Acts, alluded to above) which led him to this daring leap
from the conception of the Christians as *nourished by* the
body of Christ to this conception of their actually *being*
Christ's Body.[1] On the other hand, it is possible to point to
John ii. 21 and Heb. x. 5, 10, as hints that the idea possibly
flowed also in other than Pauline streams of thought.
Indeed, there are sayings of Jesus in the Gospels which
point in the same direction: Matt. x. 40 'He that receiveth
you receiveth me...'; xxv. 40 'Inasmuch as ye did it unto
one of these my brethren, even these least, ye did it unto
me'; Luke x. 16 'He that heareth you heareth me...';
John xiii. 20 '...he that receiveth whomsoever I send
receiveth me...'.[2]

But whatever may be thought about the origin of the
idea, it is true at any rate that it is more clearly expressed
by St Paul than by any other New Testament writer. And
it is of far-reaching importance. That the crucified Nazarene
could be spoken of as including in his Body (or Person)
all his followers is a most startling witness to his divine
status—in itself a very striking christology. And it bears
witness to the characteristic quality of Christianity which
does full justice to the individual, yet not in isolation, but
precisely because he is part of an organism and is related to
his fellow-limbs in the one body. This conception is the best
starting-point for thought and prayer about the unity of
Christians. As for the word ἐκκλησία (see pp. 154f.), it is
comprehensively used in Colossians and Ephesians as co-
extensive with the whole Body of Christ—the Church
universal. But it is still capable also of retaining its local
sense of 'congregation' (iv. 15). In i. 2, iii. 12 (see notes)
the Christians are spoken of in terms of the People of God—
another conception vitally important for the understanding

[1] See Robinson, *The Body*, especially p. 58; Mersch, *The Whole Christ*,
especially pp. vii, 80 ff.; Bonsirven, *Paul*, p. 215.
[2] So Dodd, *F.G.*, pp. 244, 418 n. 1; in the latter alluding also to
Albert Schweitzer's *Mysticism*, pp. 108 f.

7

of the nature of the Church. What of the organization of the local Church under constitutional leadership? That is not alluded to, unless it be in iv. 17. Much obscurity surrounds the early history of the ordained Ministry, and Colossians does not do much to dispel it. But we do get a glimpse in this letter of the Church at worship—singing, giving thanks to God, praying, and giving mutual instruction, much as in I Cor. xiv.

3. BECOMING A CHRISTIAN

Another great subject which emerges, even though incidentally and without premeditated design, is *the process of becoming, and the meaning of being, a Christian.* St Paul describes this in terms of being made like Christ—assimilation; not, however, by one's own efforts to copy him, but in virtue of what Christ has done: Christ's obedience to God's will is made ours. He went to the furthest limit of obedience: he parted with his very body—he stripped it off. Thereby he received it back again. He died, but he rose; he was immersed in the waters of death, but he emerged. Now the Christian rite of initiation is also an immersion and an emerging. Baptism is death to self and resurrection to God. It is a stripping off of self—it means divesting oneself of the 'old clothes' and an investiture with the new. But all this is possible, not as one's own effort, but only as one accepts incorporation in Christ. To express this idea of incorporation, St Paul uses all the symbolism of baptism (reinforced by the symbolism of circumcision, the Jewish sacrament of initiation); but also he makes powerful use of the verbs compounded with συν-: death with Christ, burial with him, resurrection with him, life with him. In short, we have come again to the organic terms of the Body of Christ.

Incorporation, in the Christian sense, means no mere imitation or following of Christ, still less mere enrolling as a member of a society: it is membership in a vividly organic

8

sense—it means becoming the living tissues of a living organism. Nobody so vividly as St Paul urges the reality of the Christian's connexion with Christ as an already accomplished fact; and in the epistles to Colossae and to the Ephesians in particular, baptized believers are described as already raised from death with Christ (see on ii. 12)—a phase of thought not exactly found elsewhere. Does such language perplex? It can be elucidated only by experience, though there are other aspects of the matter, and some further light is thrown in Galatians and Romans, where the response of trust—'justification by faith'—is stressed. Here, in Colossians, πιστεύειν does not actually occur, and πίστις only some five times, though the idea of committal to God in Christ is present. Harking back, for a moment, to the futility of mere effort without the incorporation, it is germane to this theme that, in his polemic against a spurious type of religion apparently claiming to be Christian, St Paul launches a classic attack (ii. 16–iii. 4) upon humanly devised and self-imposed religious practices, including asceticism as practised for the wrong motives. How hard the apostle can be upon himself for the right motives, and what rigours may be incurred in the Christian life, is made clear enough in I Cor. ix. 24–7. But the Colossians passage ruthlessly exposes the futility of rigours devised for their own sake, or from superstitious reasons, or by arbitrary human decision. There is all the difference in the world between undertaking 'mortifications' in the hope of becoming thereby meritorious, and, on the other hand, obeying the will of God, whether it is pleasant or unpleasant, out of love for him and in the power derived from incorporation. Only this latter is real religion. As a means to such an end, self-discipline finds its proper and inevitable place: but never as a means to deserving well of God. Hence the importance of observing precisely what 'mortify' (iii. 5) does and does not mean.

9

4. PRAYER

On *the nature and scope of Christian prayer* there is much to be learnt from Colossians. An attempt is made in the notes on i. 3–14 to indicate some of its teaching; but perhaps it is worth while to add here that the general nature of the prayer examined in those notes must not be thought to suggest that Christian prayer ought not also to be detailed and specific. From the Pauline Epistles themselves come examples of detailed and specific petitions, in Rom. xv. 30–3 (a specific prayer, which was not answered in that specific manner, but very differently), and in II Cor. xii. 8 (again, how much more profoundly answered than the petitioner had at the time imagined!).

5. ETHICS

Regarding *Christian conduct*, important deductions are drawn towards the end of Colossians, and the notes show some of their implications. But of all the ethical problems confronting Christians, in the Lycus valley and everywhere in the world of those days, that of *slavery* is the one most prominent in Colossians and Philemon together. Much has been written both about slavery in the ancient world and about the Christian attitude to it.[1] Here it may be said, first, that although the worst atrocities and barbarisms perpetrated by slave-owners may have been comparatively rare, yet the fact remains that, even at its most humane, the institution of slavery was itself incompatible with belief in the right of an individual to be treated as an end in himself

---

[1] Besides the commentaries on Philemon, see W. E. H. Lecky, *History of European Morals* (London, 1911); R. H. Barrow, *Slavery in the Roman Empire* (London, 1928); H. Wallon, *Histoire de l'esclavage dans l'antiquité* (2nd ed., Paris, 1879); Goodenough, 'P. and O.', pp. 181 ff.; Preiss, *Life in Christ*, ch. II. For some of these references I am indebted to J. Knox's *Philemon*.

and not as a mere tool or a means to an end. To claim ownership of human property is a contradiction of this belief, however tenderly the property may be used. Hence the fine protest of Stoicism[1] against slavery on the grounds of humanity. Judaism, too, had done much to mitigate slavery, as one might expect from the Hebrew idea of God. Although Ecclus. xxxiii. 24–9, 30f., xlii. 5b makes depressing reading, it is by no means the only voice of Judaism on the matter. There is, for instance, Philo's account of the Essenes:[2] '...they denounce the owners of slaves, not merely for their injustice in outraging the law of equality but also for their impiety in annulling the Statute of Nature, who motherlike has borne and reared all men alike, and created them genuine brothers, not in mere name but in genuine reality'.[3]

But it was Christianity which first transformed the relationship between master and slave so completely as to apply an explosive charge to the whole institution. The attempt had sometimes been made to destroy it by physical violence. Some formidable slave risings figure in the history of the Roman Empire,[4] as do the wholesale crucifixions and other reprisals which followed. And sometimes the leader of such an insurrection may have had the heroic quality of a martyr.[5] But it requires more than courage and physical force to explode the selfish desire for power over another's person. Only the worship of God as the Father of our Lord

[1] Chiefly, it would seem, in Seneca and his successors (i.e. chiefly in the Christian era). References in Wallon, *op. cit.* iii, pp. 49 ff.

[2] A Jewish monastic sect; see below, p. 31.

[3] *Quod Omnis Prob.* 79, trans. Dupont-Sommer, pp. 78 f.; cf. *de Vit. Contempl.* 70; and Wisdom vii. 1–6.

[4] In 73–71 B.C. Spartacus 'led the revolt of gladiators and slaves; there had been two previous wars 134–131 B.C. and 103–100 B.C.' (C. E. Raven, *Experience and Interpretation* (Gifford Lectures, ii, Cambridge, 1953), p. 93 n. 2). See also *Encycl. Brit. s.v.* Slavery; and Wallon, *op. cit.* ii, 279 ff.

[5] See Naomi Mitchison, *The Blood of the Martyrs* (London, 1939), pp. 176 f., a striking novel about Christians in Neronian Rome.

Jesus Christ possessed that secret force; and the letter to Philemon gives us a close-up view of it at work.[1] But why, then, was the force so portentously slow in acting? Even under Justinian, the mitigating laws were still strictly limited in scope; and as recently as the nineteenth century, the majority of Christians were still blind to the wickedness of the institution.[2]

The answer is, in the first place, that in a secular state, like the early Roman Empire, no change in the actual constitution could have been made by the Christians without the use of physical violence; and against this they were continually admonished. It was emphatically the Christian duty to be patient and law-abiding, even under the greatest personal injuries.[3] It was not simply the best policy, then— it was the only policy to apply the far more subtle solvent of the transformation of character. And that is necessarily a slow method. That the solvent worked far too slowly and fitfully, and that it still had not worked entirely as recently as the nineteenth century, is precisely one of those features of collective Christianity which, however deplorable, are familiar. Diffused, general Christianity often leaves patches of the public conscience quite unpenetrated. This constitutes a warning and a challenge to individuals to be alive to what God is saying. In the present day the blind spots seem to be the widespread acquiescence in the virtual slavery of industrial conditions and in the existence of war.

[1] On a wider front than merely that of the slave-master relation, the same principle is attested by such verses as Col. iii. 11, Gal. iii. 28.

[2] See Radford, pp. 341–4.

[3] I Cor. vii. 21, Eph. vi. 5–8, Col. iii. 22–24, I Tim. vi. 1 f., Titus ii. 9 f., I Pet. ii. 18–20.

II. THE CIRCUMSTANCES WHICH LED TO THE WRITING OF THE EPISTLES TO THE COLOSSIANS AND TO PHILEMON

I. AUTHORSHIP

Long ago the authenticity of Colossians and Philemon as Pauline letters was questioned, and there are still notable scholars to-day who entertain such doubts.[1] But it seems to me impossible to doubt that Philemon was written by St Paul, or to doubt the close connexion between Philemon and Colossians. At most, then, an original Pauline Colossians may have been interpolated by some writer other than St Paul: this is the only real question. And since the main criteria in this matter are contents and vocabulary, a decision turns largely (see Dibelius, p. 53) on whether or not one can imagine the type of error implied by Colossians having appeared already in St Paul's lifetime, and can conceive of St Paul dealing with it in this way and in these words. For my part, I find no serious difficulty in doing so.[2] Contents, vocabulary, and elevated style are all explainable by the circumstances:[3] the Colossian error is, as will soon

[1] F. C. Baur, over a hundred years ago, was among the earlier sceptics on this matter. More recently may be named (among others) Reitzenstein, Wendland, Schlier, Käsemann, Bultmann (see the list in E. Percy, *Probleme*, p. 6), Bornkamm (*Ende*, p. 139 n. 1), and—for parts of Colossians—Masson, and Harrison, 'O. and P.', pp. 272 ff.

[2] See the notes, especially on i. 15–23 and 24. The only expression which (according to Percy, *Probleme*, p. 46) is unparalleled in the recognized Paulines is the ὅ ἐστιν (out of strict grammatical construction; so also Eph. v. 5) of Col. iii. 14 (so many uncials; the late MSS. in general have ἥτις ἐστίν). See further the valuable discussion in Moffatt, *I.L.N.T.*, pp. 153 ff.

[3] As Lohmeyer, pp. 10 ff., observes; and see also Percy, *Probleme* pp. 40, 66, 135 f.

be shown, easily imaginable as early as St Paul's lifetime; and Paul, the martyr-apostle, is addressing unknown Christians in solemn tone about this menace. It must be added that, if Ephesians is shown to be unpauline, this in itself will not carry the same conclusion for Colossians, since the relation between Ephesians and Colossians, although close, is by no means circumstantially the same as that between Colossians and Philemon.[1] In both Colossians and Philemon the writer refers to his imprisonment,[2] in both alike Onesimus figures, and Archippus is alluded to among the recipients of greetings or messages; in both, Timothy, Aristarchus, Epaphras, Mark, Luke, and Demas are among the senders of greetings.

2. GOODSPEED AND KNOX ON PHILEMON

But, assuming that Colossians and Philemon are both real Pauline epistles, it still does not necessarily follow that the conventional reconstruction of their circumstances is correct; and the brilliant suggestions of Professors E. J. Goodspeed[3] and J. Knox[4] in America cannot be lightly dismissed. Starting from the letter to Philemon, Professor Knox's reading of the situation (to condense it to summary form, which does all too little justice to his fascinating detective story) is something like this: Philemon, he holds, may well have been overseer of the Lycus valley churches,

---

[1] Percy, *Probleme*, may have tried to prove too much in championing Ephesians also.

[2] Goodenough, 'P. and O.', questions whether δέσμιος ought not to be taken metaphorically (like δοῦλος, and cf. the note on συναιχμάλωτος, Col. iv. 10); but Col. iv. 3, let alone references in other epistles, makes this impossible. To argue, as G. does, that Paul, as a prisoner, could not have 'offered to go bond for Onesimus' peculations' seems to be to treat the situation on too rigidly legal lines. The apostle is only saying that he undertakes to pay anything that is owing.

[3] *New Solutions* and *Meaning of Eph.*

[4] *Philemon* and *Marcion*.

in succession to Epaphras—in which case he probably lived not at Colossae but at Laodicea,[1] the most important of these towns. Archippus was in some sense a patron of Christian work, though not necessarily an active evangelist. He lived at Colossae—indeed, his house-church, Philem. 2, was the Colossian church—and *he was the owner of the slave Onesimus*. For there is nothing in Philemon, Professor Knox holds, to compel one to assume, as is generally assumed, that Philemon was the owner. Now Paul, desiring to have Onesimus not only pardoned for running away but also released from slavery for work as an evangelist, sends him back to his owner, Archippus, with this covering letter which *we* now call 'to Philemon'. But he sends him *via* Philemon at Laodicea (whom he therefore includes in the greeting, Philem. 1, although it is Archippus and his church who are the main recipients), in order to win the backing of that reliable church-leader. From Philemon at Laodicea, Onesimus and the letter are to proceed to Archippus at Colossae, where this special letter, as well as the general one to the Colossians, is to be read out to the church. Moreover, it is nothing other than our so-called letter to Philemon which is alluded to in Col. iv. 16 as 'that from Laodicea'; and the 'ministry' or 'service' ($\delta\iota\alpha\kappa o\nu\iota\alpha$) which Archippus is bidden fulfil (iv. 17) is precisely that of acceding to the apostle's request about Onesimus.[2] Further, it is on these assumptions that an explanation is found, Professor Knox argues, for the striking fact that in the letter of Ignatius of Antioch to the Ephesians, in the early years of the second century A.D., one Onesimus is mentioned in a context in

---

[1] Here Goodspeed agrees. But Goodspeed, unlike Knox, places Archippus at Laodicea. Archippus, he maintains, is addressed (Col. iv. 17) as though *not* at Colossae; and Philemon and Archippus belong together (see *Meaning of Eph.*, p. 8, n. 5). For his method of bringing Col. iv. 9 into line, see below, p. 16, n. 2.

[2] For an earlier suggestion to this effect, see Moffatt, *I.L.N.T.*, p. 157.

which there are a number of remarkable echoes of the
letter to Philemon, including the following:

Philem. *vv.* 10f.	Ignatius, *Ephes.* i. 1.
...περὶ τοῦ ἐμοῦ τέκνου, ὃν ἐγέννησα ἐν τοῖς δεσμοῖς[1] Ὀνήσιμον ('...whom I have begotten as O.'—see commentary *in loc.*).	...ἀναζωπυρήσαντες ἐν αἵματι Θεοῦ τὸ συγγενικὸν ἔργον τελείως ἀπηρτίσατε...(which, Knox thinks, is a reference to the '*congenital*' name of the church's representative Onesimus).

Knox therefore suggests that it is far from fantastic to see
in Ignatius' Onesimus, not some other bearer of the same
name, but the released slave himself, fulfilling his promise;
and, indeed, to ascribe to Onesimus a leading part in the
collecting of the Pauline epistles, including the 'letter to
Philemon' which so closely concerned himself. It is at this
point that Knox's conjectures link up with those of Professor Goodspeed on the origin of the Pauline *corpus* of
collected letters, and the nature of the Epistle to the
Ephesians as the collector's 'covering letter' to the whole
corpus. This latter question would take us into a field belonging rather to the commentator on Ephesians; but, confining
ourselves to the present epistles, I find it almost impossible,
for my part, to interpret Archippus' 'ministry' (an active
word) in Col. iv. 17 as simply the giving up of Onesimus for
Christian service, especially when the verb is better suited
to something 'handed on', as by tradition (ἣν παρέλαβες ἐν
Κυρίῳ). Rather, it must surely be some function in the
Church, which had been entrusted to him. And if so, there
is no very cogent reason for associating the slave with
Archippus rather than (as is usually done) with Philemon,
or for removing Philemon to Laodicea from Colossae, where
Onesimus belonged (Col. iv. 9).[2] Indeed, the facts that

---

[1] Omitting the usually printed comma.

[2] Goodspeed has to do some special pleading (*Meaning of Eph.*, p. 8,
n. 5) to show that ὁ ἐξ ὑμῶν (Col. iv. 9) merely means 'who belongs to
the Lycus valley', or, at most, 'who *originally* came from Colossae' (see

16

Philemon is the first person addressed in the letter, and that, after the additional names, the phrase κατ' οἶκόν σου (singular) is used (v. 2), seem to be fatal to the theory that Archippus is primarily the one addressed. It is one person—the first named—who is addressed throughout. That Archippus lives in a different town from Philemon's is correspondingly ruled out. If this is granted, then the epistle was to Philemon and apparently went straight to him at Colossae (not *via* him at Laodicea to Archippus at Colossae),[1] and it becomes necessary to identify the letter from Laodicea of Col. iv. 16 otherwise.

This, however, constitutes the real problem confronting the conventional reconstruction of the circumstances. Why should this important letter have been lost, whereas Colossians and the apparently much less important Philemon have survived? And it is the suggestion that Philemon should be identified with the lost letter which must count as the most striking and important part of the theories of Goodspeed and Knox. For the details of their case the reader is referred to their books. But it must still be said that Col. iv. 16 requires to be rather severely strained to fit their meaning; for what is contemplated in that verse is manifestly an *exchange* of letters: καὶ ὅταν ἀναγνωσθῇ παρ' ὑμῖν ἡ ἐπιστολή, ποιήσατε ἵνα καὶ ἐν τῇ Λαοδικέων ἐκκλησίᾳ

---

below, p. 19, n. 2). Goodspeed, unlike Knox, places not only Philemon but also Archippus and Onesimus at Laodicea. Like Knox, he regards the letter to Philemon as identical with the letter from Laodicea of Col. iv. 16. Regarding iv. 17, he says that 'tell Archippus, etc.' 'sounds as though Archippus were at Laodicea and, if he was, "Philemon" was sent to that place' (*New Solutions*, p. 51; cf. *Meaning of Eph.*, p. 6). He thinks that Philemon stood in the original collection of Pauline letters as 'Laodiceans'; that then Laodicea fell into disrepute (Rev. iii. 16), and this letter was therefore *called* 'Philemon', thus reducing the letters named after *Churches* to only six; and that then, later still, the number was made up to seven again by Ephesians coming in *as* 'Laodiceans'. Marcion called Ephesians 'Laodiceans' because (on this showing) he knew that in the list there had been a 'Laodiceans' but not an 'Ephesians'.

[1] Theodoret *in Philem.* (for what his witness is worth) says that Philemon's house in Colossae μέχρι τοῦ παρόντος μεμένηκε.

17

ἀναγνωσθῇ, καὶ τὴν ἐκ Λαοδικίας ἵνα καὶ ὑμεῖς ἀναγνῶτε. In view of the first part of the verse, one would be bound to assume, unless there were the strongest reasons to the contrary, that the letter alluded to in the second part of it was *addressed primarily to Laodicea*—just as Colossians was to Colossae—and was to be passed on from Laodicea to Colossae, just as Colossians was to be passed on from Colossae to Laodicea and itself contained greetings to the Laodicene Church (Col. iv. 15).[1] It is well known that Marcion (the heretic, about A.D. 150) spoke of what we call Ephesians as the letter to the Laodiceans, and that Philemon was also in his 'canon'.[2] He at least, therefore, seems to have thought in terms of a letter to Laodicea *and* a letter to Philemon besides.[3] Incidentally, a so-called Letter to the Laodiceans is extant in Latin in certain MSS. but it is universally agreed to be a forgery (such as, indeed, is alluded to in the Muratorian Canon). It is printed by, among others, Lightfoot in his commentary on Colossians, by Westcott,[4] and, in an English translation, by M. R. James.[5]

3. ALTERNATIVE VIEWS

If, then, we are not convinced by this very ingenious rehandling of the theme, we must revert to some form of the more conventional view.[6]

[1] There are three readings here: (1) τὴν κατ᾽ οἶκον αὐτῆς ἐκκλησίαν, (2) ...αὐτοῦ..., (3) ...αὐτῶν.... The plural is the least likely to be original. See below, p. 28, n. 1.   [2] See Tertullian, *adv. Marc.*

[3] For Goodspeed's explanation of this, see above, p. 16, n. 2.

[4] *The Canon of the New Testament* (London, 1875).

[5] *The Apocryphal New Testament* (Oxford, 1924), pp. 479f. Harrison, 'O. and P.', pp. 284ff., accepting the Ephesian imprisonment theory (see below, pp. 21 ff.), hazards the guess that the original Laodicean letter was destroyed in the earthquake of A.D. 60, and that Ephesians was written to fill the gap.

[6] In passing, it is worth while to remark that, in any case, even if Goodspeed and Knox are not accepted, it is misleading to describe Philemon, as it is sometimes described, as merely 'a personal note'. It is true that Jerome (*Preface to Philemon*) and Tertullian (*adv. Marc.* v. 21) both refer to disparaging estimates of it, as Knox himself points out

As ordinarily reconstructed, the circumstances were that Philemon's slave, Onesimus, had run away, apparently with stolen money (Philem. 18).[1] He had somehow met St Paul in prison and had, apparently, been brought by him to accept Christianity, or to return to it after a lapse.[2] Now he is sent back to his master with this letter from the apostle, which was carried, it seems, by Tychicus (Col. iv. 7).

How did Onesimus meet St Paul, or, as Theodoret puts it (in his commentary), fall into the apostolic net? If, after running away, he had been caught, he would simply have

(*Philemon*, p. 46), as brief or as merely individual and not ecclesiastical. But in fact it is addressed not to one person only, but to three, and to a church—a 'house-church' or a community which belongs in Philemon's home or meets in his house. And it is considerably longer than the average letter, to judge by the surviving specimens (see Roller, *Formular*, especially pp. 40, 360 ff.). The famous letter from the younger Pliny (*Ep.* ix. 21), urging a friend to grant pardon to a slave, is less than half the length of Philemon (149 against 335 words). Some of the various statements which are appended to the epistles in certain manuscripts of the New Testament, embodying traditions or speculations about their destination and so forth, describe this letter, with a touch of formality, as addressed to Philemon and Apphia and Archippus, the deacon of the Church at Colossae (a deduction, no doubt, from Col. iv. 17). Perhaps it is right to add, with Preiss (*Life in Christ*, pp. 33 f.), that in the 'new age', the age of Christianity, an intensely individual and private matter becomes something to be *shared*, just as, conversely, nothing is so collective as not to remain genuinely 'personal'. If so, it has, however, to be admitted that the second and third epistles of John seem to be absolutely individual.   [1] See *Appendix*, pp. 34 ff.

[2] Philem. 10, 16; and cf. Col. iv. 9, describing him as the trustworthy and loved brother. Goodspeed (*Meaning of Eph.*, p. 8, n. 5) argues that ὁ ἐξ ὑμῶν cannot mean that O. was a member of the Colossian *church* [presumably on the assumption that, until he met St Paul, he was not a Christian at all]; and that, therefore, it is arbitrary to limit the ὑμεῖς to the *city* of Colossae, and easy to make it mean inhabitants of the Lycus valley. But if he can now be described as the trustworthy and loved brother (i.e. a Christian), then *ipso facto* ἐξ ὑμῶν may mean ' (now) belonging to your (Christian) community'; and that means, most naturally, the one at *Colossae*. That St Paul can be explicit when he wishes a single message to include more than a single community or city is shown by I Cor. i. 2, II Cor. i. 1, Gal. i. 2. These inclusive greetings may be contrasted with the specific address in Col. i. 2 to God's people *at Colossae*; and this latter type of address (including also Rom. i. 6, Phil. i. 1, I Thess. i. 1, v. 27, II Thess. i. 1) may be contrasted, in turn, with Philem. 1, 2, limiting the address to a house-community.

been returned to Philemon. If he had taken asylum at some heathen shrine such as offered temporary protection or in some heathen family and refused to go back to Philemon, he would have been sold to some other master.[1] In neither case would he have met St Paul, unless, by some strange fortune, he had chanced to be imprisoned in the same prison with him.[2] If so, we must suppose that he was released on parole, as a result of St Paul's guarantee that he would return to his master. It seems more likely that he had previously met St Paul with Philemon. He might even have heard the apostle expounding the Christian faith (Philem. 19 suggests that Philemon owed his conversion to St Paul), and have been led by the memory of this to go and seek out a man whom he believed to be able to help him now in his need.[3] In fact, he may have taken asylum with St Paul,[4] supposing always that St Paul's imprisonment was of a lax sort admitting free access (cf. Acts xxiv. 23, xxviii. 16, 30). Such a theory demands that Philemon himself must have met Paul somewhere outside the Lycus valley, where Paul was not known personally (Col. ii. 2); and we may guess that it was during a visit to Ephesus. Like Epaphras, he may have gone to and fro between Paul and his home. In Philem. 1 he is described as a fellow-worker with the apostle.

Be that as it may, St Paul is now in a position to make big demands on Philemon, and he might have taken advantage of this to keep Onesimus with him (v. 13). But, strictly speaking, it was defrauding a master to retain his runaway slave, whose services were owed to the master; and, besides, the

[1] References to Hellenic slave law may be found in Goodenough, 'P. and O.'. See also Wilcken (as in Appendix, p. 34), p. 571.

[2] A guess hazarded by P. S. Minear, *The Kingdom and the Power* (Philadelphia, 1950), p. 202.

[3] Epaphras belonged to the Lycus valley, but was now in the same place as St Paul (Col. iv. 12). Perhaps he was the link between Onesimus and St Paul. See Harrison, 'O. and P.', p. 272.

[4] Lohmeyer, p. 172; Rendtorff.

Christian view of a proper relation between persons required that the breach between master and slave should not be acquiesced in but repaired by bravely grasping the nettle of repentance and forgiveness. Therefore Onesimus is sent back, to straighten out the situation, with the friendly help, no doubt, of Tychicus and the weighty backing of this cogent letter.

Did St Paul expect Philemon to waive his right to Onesimus and release him? Professor J. Knox takes the παρακαλῶ σε περί...of v. 10 to mean 'I request you for...', as though Paul were not making a request *concerning* Onesimus but rather *for the gift of him*—asking to have him permanently as a helper in his work. Whether that is so or not, it is evident that, although the apostle contemplates the possibility that Philemon might see fit to retain him (v. 15), yet he hopes that he may release him (vv. 14, 21). If so, it would not be merely to wait on him in prison; for, although that was Paul's immediate need (v. 13), he evidently expected to be released before long (v. 22). It must, then, have been for some other purpose—possibly, as Professor Knox surmises, as an active evangelist or assistant in evangelism. There seems to be no cogent reason against the identification of the freed slave with the bishop of the same name addressed by Ignatius. We have already seen Professor Knox urging this view (above, p. 16); and Harrison ('O. and P.', pp. 290 f.) seems to be justified in challenging Lightfoot's contention that Ignatius seems to be 'speaking of a person comparatively young and untried in office'. It is thus possible, though not demonstrable, that we are given a glimpse of a spectacular sequel to St Paul's letter many years later.

4. WHERE WAS ST PAUL?

But it is time to ask the inevitable question: Where was Paul in prison? The 'subscriptions' to the epistles which appear in various MSS. (already alluded to above, p. 18,

n. 6) probably represent nothing more than the guesses of scribes or commentators based on the contents of the epistles themselves; but, for what they are worth, they unanimously assume what seems, until modern times, seldom to have been doubted—that Colossians and Philemon (as also Philippians and Ephesians, the other 'captivity Epistles'—though Ephesians had no 'subscription') were written by Paul from prison at Rome. This would mean that they were among his latest writings, to be dated about A.D. 60 or a little later. This date would hold good within a narrow margin, whether or not two Roman imprisonments were postulated. However, already in the time of Marcion (second century) there appear to have been some who doubted this; for the so-called Monarchian Prologues (believed to be connected with Marcion himself) describe Colossians as written from Ephesus,[1] although they assign both Philippians and Philemon to Rome—the latter very strangely, considering how closely Philemon and Colossians cohere. It was left for commentators of the modern period to take up this hint, and to ask whether the assumption that Colossians and the other prison epistles were written from Rome was correct.

It was pointed out by Erich Haupt in 1902—if not by an earlier scholar—that we know from Acts xxiii. 33–xxvi. 32 of a prolonged imprisonment undergone by St Paul at Caesarea while he was awaiting trial. Might not this be the place of origin of the captivity epistles? The companions whom Colossians and Philemon show to have been with St Paul at the time of writing are not incompatible with what

[1] The Prologue in question runs: 'AD COLOSSENSES. Colossenses et hi sicut Laudicenses sunt Asiani, et ipsi praeventi erant a pseudapostolis nec ad hos accessit ipse apostolus, sed et hos per epistulam recorrigit—audierant enim verbum ab Archippo qui et ministerium in eos accepit—ergo apostolus iam ligatus scribit eis ab Epheso.' The Prologues were discussed in a famous article by Dom D. de Bruyne in *Revue bénédictine* xxiv (1907), pp. 1–16; and are to be found, in Latin and/or English, in F. C. Burkitt's *The Gospel History and its Transmission* (Edinburgh, 1907), J. Knox's *Marcion*, and A. Souter's *The Text and Canon of the N.T.* (London, 1912).

we know of the Caesarea period, and the suggestion seems plausible (especially since the Lycus valley is nearer to Caesarea than to Rome), except in one important respect. That is, that St Paul must have known, during his imprisonment at Caesarea, that to be released would inevitably mean being lynched by the Jews, and that his one hope of remaining alive was to go to Rome under Roman escort (see Acts xxiii. 11–23, xxviii. 17, 18). This is incompatible with his expectations of release in Philem. 22. It may be added that Col. iv. 3, though giving little indication as to locality, looks similar to Phil. i. 13—wherever Philippians is deemed to have been written; and that in Phil. i. 25, ii. 24 expectations of release are also expressed.[1]

But why not, then, it has been asked,[2] assume an imprisonment at Ephesus? It was the apostle's base during the so-called 'third journey' (Acts xix). It is demonstrable, by comparing II Cor. xi. 23–7 with Acts, that the Acts narrative is no exhaustive account of all his adventures; and further hints are detected by some in Rom. xvi. 4, I Cor. xv. 32, II Cor. i. 8–11. Moreover, there is the phrase, already alluded to, in the Monarchian Prologue to Colossians;[3] and among the ruins at Ephesus is a building which local tradition still calls St Paul's prison.

Applying alike to Caesarea and Ephesus are the arguments from proximity and from date. A runaway slave, it is urged, would be more likely to reach Ephesus or Caesarea than distant Rome. The journeying to and fro implied by Philippians (if that letter belongs to this group) suggests a distance shorter than that between Rome and Greece, not

[1] Despite this obstacle, the Caesarea hypothesis has been, and continues to be, held by some—notably, among recent scholars, in Dibelius and Kümmel's *St Paul* (London, 1953), and by Lohmeyer.

[2] See, especially, G. S. Duncan, *St Paul's Ephesian Ministry* (London, 1929), and C. R. Bowen in *A.J.T.*, vol. xxiv (1920).

[3] But the *iam* suggests that the writer somehow thought that the imprisonment in question was a preliminary part of one long, continuous imprisonment. Did he imagine that St Paul called at Ephesus *on the way to Rome*?

to mention inland Asia Minor. It would have been absurd
to write from Rome asking for hospitality in the Lycus
valley (Philem. 22), especially when the apostle's plan had
been to go on from Rome to Spain (Rom. xv. 24). And as
for date, the phrases in Colossians, it is said, suit best a
recently founded Church;[1] and the phrase in Phil. iv. 10
about the Philippians having had no opportunity to contribute to St Paul's needs would be little short of sarcastic if it
were written at about A.D. 60, but quite natural at the
Ephesus or Caesarea period. It must be said in parenthesis
that if Ephesians is Pauline, and if it was originally directed
to the Church at Ephesus, then of course it has to be
dissociated from the other captivity letters by those who
hold that they were written *from* Ephesus. But the 'if' is, in
both cases, a notoriously big one.

In view of these arguments, Ephesus is not to be lightly
dismissed. Yet the case for Rome is still a strong one, and—
so it seems to the present writer—on the whole more
plausible than the others. After all, evidence for an
Ephesian imprisonment is dubious, whereas for Rome it is
convincing. Luke, who was with St Paul when Colossians
and Philemon were written (Col. iv. 14, Philem. 24),
appears *not* to have joined him by the Ephesus period (for
no 'we'-passages occur in Acts between xvi. 17 and xx. 5).
Travel between Rome and the east was frequent and not so
formidable a task as to make the communications implied
by the captivity epistles impossible. A runaway slave might
well make for Rome on the principle that the metropolis of
the empire is the easiest place to hide in. And, as C. H.
Dodd has ingeniously argued,[2] the phrase in Philippians
about the lack of opportunity to contribute to St Paul's
needs may be explained by the necessity felt by him to

---

[1] So C. R. Bowen, *J.B.L.*, vol. XLIII (1924), pp. 189f.
[2] 'The Mind of Paul: Change and Development', in *B.J.R.L.*, vol. XVIII,
no. 1 (Jan. 1934), p. 83.

refuse personal gifts during the period while he was engaged on raising money for the relief of the poor Jewish Christians, for fear of incurring suspicion for embezzlement. Finally, against C. R. Bowen's contention, alluded to above, that Colossians implies a recently founded Church, there is the fact that, at any rate, sufficient time must be allowed for the error which is attacked in this letter to have developed. These considerations perhaps just tip the scale in favour of Rome as the place of origin.

5. ST PAUL'S FRIENDS

Whatever uncertainty attaches to St Paul's whereabouts, at least Colossians and Philemon enable us to draw up a list of his companions at the time of writing. The following are mentioned by name: Timothy (Col. i. 1, Philem. 1), Aristarchus, Mark, Jesus Justus, Epaphras, Luke, Demas, Tychicus, and Onesimus (Col. iv. 7-14, Philem. 10, 23, 24). Of these, Timothy is known, from Acts xvi. 1-3, to have been a Jewish Christian, and Aristarchus, Mark, and Jesus Justus are so described in Col. iv. The same passage shows that the others were Gentiles. We know nothing (unless by indirect means) about Jesus Justus; nor about Demas, unless he be identified with the unfaithful Demas of II Tim. iv. 10 (who is there also associated with Luke and Mark). About Timothy, Mark, and Luke a good deal can be gathered from the New Testament. Timothy was a particularly intimate and valued companion and assistant of St Paul's, and—according to I and II Timothy at least—was ordained to office in the Church: he is an interesting example of a 'second-generation' Christian, who had had a Christian upbringing. Whether it is the same Timothy who also appears in Hebrews, it is impossible to say.[1]

[1] See Acts xvi. 1 ff., xvii. 14, 15, xviii. 5, xix. 22, xx. 4, Rom. xvi. 21, I Cor. iv. 17, xvi. 10, II Cor. i. 1, 19, Phil. i. 1, ii. 19-22, Col. i. 1, I Thess. i. 1, iii. 2, 6, II Thess. i. 1, I Tim. i. 1 ff., vi. 20, II Tim. i. 1 ff., Philem. 1, Heb. xiii. 23.

Of Mark, if all the occurrences of his name are assumed to apply to one and the same person, we know that he was a cousin to Barnabas (Col. iv. 10), who was himself a Levite of Cyprus (Acts iv. 36); that his home was in Jerusalem (Acts xii. 12, 25); that he incurred St Paul's censure for retreating from the 'first journey', and thereafter went with Barnabas to Cyprus (Acts xiii. 13, xv. 37–9); but that he seems to have been welcomed back ultimately into favour (Col. iv. 10, Philem. 24, II Tim. iv. 11). The name appears also in I Pet. v. 13. In Acts he always appears bearing, as his primary name, John. What is the precise connexion—if any—of John Mark with the Gospel according to St Mark is a matter which cannot here be discussed.[1] But it is very interesting to speculate upon two evangelists having personal, and not merely literary, contact, in the company of St Paul: for next comes Luke.

Luke is described in Col. iv. 14 as 'the doctor, our dear friend', and is, as has already been said, among the Gentiles in that passage. Philem. 24 and II Tim. iv. 11 are the only other allusions to him by name in the New Testament; but a tradition which there is no reason to doubt associates his name with a Gospel, and the opening words of Acts associate Acts and Gospel together, as two parts of a single work. There is strong reason, therefore, to see in Luke the only known Gentile writer of Scripture. If the 'we-passages' in Acts are by the writer of the remainder of the book, then Luke is further shown to have been a fellow-traveller with St Paul at certain definite stages.

Aristarchus was a Macedonian of Thessalonica, and shared St Paul's last journey to Jerusalem and the journey to Rome (Acts xix. 29, xx. 4, xxvii. 2). The term συναιχμάλω-τος in Col. iv. 10 is probably not, however, to be taken as a

[1] For extra-biblical evidence, see the commentaries on Mark; and for suggestions for dissociating the Evangelist from the Jerusalemite Mark, see F. C. Grant, *The Earliest Gospel* (Abingdon-Cokesbury Press, 1943), and G. Dix, *Jew and Greek* (Dacre Press, 1953).

literal reference to imprisonment (see notes *in loc.*). Tychicus was from the province of Asia, and, like Aristarchus, was with St Paul on his last journey to Jerusalem (Acts xx. 4). He also appears in Eph. vi. 21 as a trusted emissary, and in II Tim. iv. 12 and Titus iii. 12. He was, as has been seen, evidently the bearer of Colossians and Philemon. Epaphras is an important figure about whom one would like to know more. He is generally distinguished from the Epaphroditus of Phil. ii. 25, iv. 18—not that the two names are not interchangeable, but because Epaphroditus evidently belonged at Philippi, whereas Epaphras is explicitly referred to in Col. iv. 12 as ὁ ἐξ ὑμῶν, belonging at Colossae. But at the time of writing, he was away from Colossae with Paul. Bieder (pp. 302 ff.) suggests that the πόνος which Epaphras is suffering (*v.* 13) is due to some serious rift between him and the Colossian Church; and that, now that he is staying away, it is his office that Archippus has 'taken over' (*v.* 17). We have already seen Professor Knox similarly suggesting Philemon as his successor. But it seems more natural to attribute this 'toil' to the mental and spiritual labour which his concern for their welfare involves, although the reason for his staying with St Paul remains obscure. St Paul himself, similarly, experienced great 'labour' in prayer and anxious concern over these communities (cf. II Cor. xi. 28f.): both he and Epaphras are putting forth energy strenuously on behalf of them (Col. ii. 1f.). It may be that Epaphras owed his conversion to St Paul. It certainly appears, from Col. i. 7[1] (cf. ii. 1), that he, in his turn, had

---

[1] Here, the reading πιστὸς ὑπὲρ ἡμῶν διάκονος τοῦ Χριστοῦ is preferable to ...ὑπὲρ ὑμῶν. ἡμῶν (that is Paul, or Paul and his associates) is read by p⁴⁶ ℵ*ABD*G (well-distributed and early witnesses), as against ὑμῶν by CKLP and many others, by lat sy and *s* (later, and not quite so widely representative a group). Throughout the epistle, there is constant doubt about the correct reading as between first and second person. Thus: in i. 12 ἡμᾶς ADG *pm s*; ὑμᾶς ℵB 69 1739 *al*. In ii. 13 ὑμᾶς (2nd) is read by the majority of those which read a pronoun there at all, but ἡμᾶς by p⁴⁶ B 1 69 *al*, while the pronoun is omitted by DGP

been, as the apostle's representative, the evangelist of Colossae—if not of Laodicea and Hierapolis also. In Philem. 23 he is called St Paul's συναιχμάλωτος, just as Aristarchus is in Col. iv. 10, and as Andronicus and Junias are in Rom. xvi. 7.

At the 'receiving end', the only Christians mentioned by name (apart from Onesimus himself and Epaphras, who, as we have seen, properly belonged there) are Nymphas,[1] Archippus (Col. iv. 17, Philem. 2), Philemon,[2] and Apphia. There were congregations or groups meeting in houses

al lat ϛ; ἡμῖν is replaced by ὑμῖν in LP 69 *al* vg ϛ. The best reading thus seems to be ὑμᾶς...ἡμῖν: Gentiles are being addressed by Paul the Jew; but Gentiles and Jews alike need forgiveness. For a much more problematic transition from second to first person, see Eph. ii. 1–10, one of the passages where Goodspeed (*Meaning of Eph.*) detects a Gentile imitator of St Paul, unsuccessfully trying to sustain the part of a Jew. See also Col. iii. 4, where ἡμῶν is read by B *al* sy ϛ, ὑμῶν by 𝔭⁴⁶𝕏DG *pm* lat arm.

[1] This—a man's name—is not the form printed by Westcott and Hort or by the Bible Society. But I adopt it for the following reasons. The question is whether the letters Νυμφαν represent the accusative of a masc. name Νυμφᾶς (a contraction of Νυμφόδωρος or the like—cf. Ἐπαφρᾶς for Ἐπαφρόδιτος and Λουκᾶς for (?) Λούκιος, etc.), or of a fem. Νύμφα. Since the oldest hands in the most ancient MSS. offer no accents (Bᶜ Or show fem., L P ϛ show masc.), the only ancient evidence lies in the personal pronoun which follows. The pronoun in the phrase τὴν κατ' οἶκον αὐτ— ἐκκλησίαν is attested thus: αὐτῆς: B 6 1739 Or; αὐτοῦ: DG *pm* ϛ; αὐτῶν: 𝕏A 1912 *al*. Of these, the plural is by no means clearly original, since it is possible (*pace* Lightfoot) to imagine a sleepy scribe altering singular to plural (however illogically) because of the impressive plurality of the preceding words. Besides, is it likely that the house belonged to them all? And the MS. support for αὐτῶν is not cogent. As between αὐτῆς and αὐτοῦ, the MS. support for the latter is admittedly not impressive; but it may well be right, as against αὐτῆς, since it is easy to imagine a scribe assuming that Νυμφαν must be a feminine, and altering the pronoun accordingly. Besides, Νύμφα (as commentators point out) is a Doric form (as against the commoner Νύμφη) and is itself unlikely in Colossae (though this does not reduce the likelihood of a later scribe thinking it a fem.); and I do not think that J. H. Moulton's argument (*Prolegomena to a Grammar of N.T. Greek*, Edinburgh, 1908, p. 48) explains this away. The question is, not Could a gen. Νύμφης ever give rise to a non-Doric nom. Νύμφᾰ? but Are the nom. and acc. Νύμφα, Νύμφαν found often enough to make it likely that this is what is intended here?

[2] A name familiar to us from the delightful tale of the aged Phrygian peasants, Baucis and Philemon, 'who entertained not angels but gods unawares' (Lightfoot, p. 304: see Ovid, *Met.* VIII. 626ff.).

(Col. iv. 15 and Philem. 2). What the διακονία of Archippus was remains uncertain, as has already been said; but it may well have been some office in the administration of the local church or of one of these house-congregations. That Philemon and Apphia were husband and wife is likely enough; and that Archippus was their son is at least possible, in view of the greetings in Philemon. Why Colossae and Laodicea are so closely associated as they are in Colossians, whereas Hierapolis, the third city of the Lycus valley trio, does not come in for more than passing mention in iv. 13, is obscure.

6. THE SITUATION ADDRESSED

That the majority of the Christians addressed were Gentiles is, as Abbott observes, what one would expect if Epaphras the Gentile was their evangelist; and it is further suggested by i. 12, 21 (probably), 27—where the terms are those of outsiders being brought inside—and ii. 13 (see above, p. 27, n. 1); also, perhaps, by the scarcity of Old Testament allusions in these letters,[1] by the distinctively Gentile vices[2] alluded to in iii. 5–7, and by the comparative paucity of references to the matter of reconciliation between the Jewish and Gentile sections of the Christian church (in marked contrast to the stress upon this in Ephesians). But there remains iii. 11 ('where there is no question of Greek and Jew...') to show that the issue was not dead even

---

[1] C. R. Bowen, *J.B.L.*, vol. XLIII (1924), p. 193, finds at most five formal reflexions of Scriptural language in Colossians: ii. 3 (Isa. xlv. 3), 22 (Isa. xxix. 13), iii. 1 (Ps. cx. 1), 10 (Gen. i. 26 f.), 25 (Deut. x. 17). On the other hand, i. 12 is full of O.T. ideas (see notes there). For a possible trace of Rabbinic methods behind i. 16 ff., see note vi (*e*) on i. 15–23, p. 62; but this does not necessarily presuppose such knowledge in the reader: it is intelligible without it.

[2] Though these might be reconciled with Judaism by postulating that some, at least, of the converts to Christianity had first been brought out of paganism into Judaism as proselytes (cf. W. C. van Unnik's suggestions to this effect regarding the recipients of I Peter (*Verlossing*)).

here; and iv. 11 also at least shows that St Paul regarded the Colossians as interested in the conflict.

One must also take into consideration the nature of the error which is attacked in ii. 4–23 and, by implication, elsewhere. What was it, and where did it spring from? It is doubtful how far it is useful to attempt a rigid contrast between distinctively Jewish and non-Jewish elements. It is possible to state what is alien to *biblical* Judaism, or what appears to be *logically* incompatible with its basic tenets. But, as a fact, strange amalgams did appear, composed of Judaism and alien elements together, exactly as amalgams of alien matter and Christianity did, and still do, appear. It is therefore unwise to assert *a priori* of any given tenet that it could not have been grafted on Judaism. However— purely as a preliminary analysis—one may sort the elements of the 'Colossian error' into the *logically* Jewish and non-Jewish, as follows:[1]

Elements found in pure Judaism, though not exclusively	Exclusively Jewish elements	Exclusively, or at least predominantly, Hellenic elements
ii. 8 ἡ παράδοσις τῶν ἀνθρώπων.	ii. 11–13 περιτομή.[2]	i. 19 etc. τὸ πλήρωμα(?).[3]
ii. 16 (cf. *v.* 21) βρῶσις, ἑορτή, νεομηνία.	ii. 16 σάββατα.	ii. 3 γνῶσις (?).[3]
		ii. 8 ἡ φιλοσοφία (?).[3]
		ii. 16 πόσις.[4]
		ii. 23 ἀφειδία σώματος.[5]

---

[1] I am here (as elsewhere) indebted not only to many published works, but also to the kindness of the Rev. W. Fenton Morley in permitting me to read and use an unpublished work of his on the Colossian error. His conclusions, even where I have not fully accepted them, have thrown fresh light at several points.

[2] See A. Lukyn-Williams, *J.T.S.* x (1909), p. 413, for the probability that in this context it could only be *Jewish* circumcision. Cf. Percy, *Probleme*, against Dibelius.

[3] But all these three are far from certainly classifiable.

[4] For the Mosaic Law says little about clean and unclean drink (see, however, Lev. xi. 34, 36, cited by Lightfoot)—unless the reference is (as in Rom. xiv) to abstinence (so Percy, *Probleme*, p. 140).

[5] Not a truly Jewish conception, see Percy, p. 141.

I have not included the δόγματα of ii. 14 under a Jewish heading, because it cannot be proved that it does not include 'decrees' wider and more general than the Mosaic Law (see notes there). It would be rash, also, to attempt to 'place' the στοιχεῖα of ii. 8, 20, until we are absolutely certain what the word means in its context. One other item, however, the cult of angels, we must consider in a moment.

Meanwhile, it must be confessed that the evidence is slender enough. But the combination of all the elements in the above analysis, and the ideas which may be deduced from the view of Christ which St Paul advances in opposition to them, certainly fit well enough into the pattern of a kind of 'theosophy'—in this instance, a 'gnostic'[1] type of Judaism or a Jewish type of 'gnosticism'. From writings later than the New Testament period there is a good deal of evidence for this sort of thing.[2] And such an amalgam is made the more likely for the Lycus valley, in that its Jewish population appears to have been considerable[3] (however few Jewish Christians there may have been in these churches), while a pagan shrine dominated the town of Colossae.[4] Moreover, we know of something not unlike this already in existence before the beginning of the Christian era—namely, the system of the monastic sect of the Essenes in Palestine. Lightfoot's famous comparison of the Colossian error with Essenism so far as it was known, chiefly from Philo and Josephus, showed how well it matched such a mixed religion, consisting of Judaism combined with alien elements (see the Excursus in his Commentary). And if the recent discoveries near the Dead Sea

[1] For Gnosticism, see A Note on the Knowledge of God, p. 159; and see The Jung Codex (there quoted), pp. 62, 75, 78.

[2] See Bornkamm, Ende, especially pp. 149f., for evidence, including that of Epiphanius, Haer. xxx. 15. 3 (vegetarian rules belonging to the δόγματα of the Ebionites).

[3] Lukyn-Williams, p. xiii; Schürer in Hastings' Dictionary of the Bible, v, pp. 93 ff.

[4] Lukyn-Williams, pp. xxxivf.

relate to Essenism, a flood of fresh light may be thrown on it, and we may the more readily agree with Lightfoot when he asks whether it is not reasonable to suppose, for the Lycus valley, something similar to this Palestinian movement.[1] Whether the sect of the Dead Sea caves was Essene or not, at any rate it was evidently in many respects a Jewish sect, yet contained elements which (on the *a priori* test) would be deemed incompatible. It is possible that the Essenes actually worshipped the sun;[2] and a similar charge might be laid against the Dead Sea sect.[3] Indeed, sun-worship had already begun to invade Judaism by the time Ezek. viii. 16 was written. If so, still less impossible is the cult of angels. Lightfoot had already pointed out that the Essenes were, at any rate, concerned with the names of angels, as were later semi-Christian sects.

Accordingly, it is difficult to say categorically 'this or that cannot be combined with the other': we have sufficient evidence of strange unions to make us cautious. We can still discuss just what role the 'cult' of angels played in the Colossian error: was it (as E. Percy, *Probleme*, would have it) only a recognition of the good Jewish idea of mediating angels, and thus simply a form of reverence for the Law? On this showing both the affirmations in Colossians and in Heb. i and ii, about the superiority of Christ to the angels, are different ways of affirming Christ's absolute superiority to the Law (Percy, pp. 175f.). Or was it something more seriously pagan—polytheism or something bordering on it? Percy (p. 140) makes an ingenious point when he maintains that it is impossible to think that St Paul would have claimed *pagan* rites as σκιὰ τῶν μελλόντων

---

[1] Dupont-Sommer strongly advocates the identification with the Essenes, and believes that they represented a movement which spread far beyond Palestine (cf. the Therapeutae in Egypt). But for a critique of D.-S.'s conclusions, see H. F. D. Sparks in *The Modern Churchman*, XLIV, no. 4 (Dec. 1954), pp. 300 ff.

[2] Josephus, *B.J.* II, § 128.

[3] Though not by Dupont-Sommer (see pp. 104 ff.).

(Col. ii. 17—'a foreshadowing of the reality to come'). But it is difficult to be certain. Perhaps we must be content to draw, as the background of Colossians, a general picture of persons who themselves apparently claimed to be Christians (cf. Percy, p. 142), however far outside Christianity some of their beliefs may actually have lain; while, at the same time, they valued a type of asceticism condemned by St Paul, gave a position to a ritual calendar and food-tabus which called out his strong opposition (contrast the gentleness of Rom. xiv, but compare Heb. xiii. 9), reverenced angels[1] (or possibly worshipped them), and set store by visions which the apostle regarded as 'bogus'. Further, it is plausibly suggested (though not demonstrable) that they conceived of salvation as a matter of conciliating or overcoming various angelic, supra-human 'Powers' or 'Influences'—star-demons, or whatever they might be—of whom Jesus was regarded by them as only one among the many who controlled the approaches to salvation. In Enoch lxi. 10, the 'Elect One' holds a similar position among the Cherubim, Seraphim, Ophannim, and so forth (see note on Col. i. 16). This would all add up to the sort of notions found perhaps in Essenism and certainly in the later 'gnostic' systems, and it would lend point to St Paul's emphasis on the entire completeness of the deity residing in Christ and all the stores of wisdom and knowledge being concealed in him. If there was a strong dualism in the error (comparable to that of the Dead Sea sect), it may be that St Paul deliberately uses their terms, for his own ends, in i. 13. But a wholesale equation of the Colossian error with the later gnostic systems is certainly a rash assumption.[2]

---

[1] Bornkamm, *Ende*, p. 149, cites the Book of Elkasai (in Hippolytus, *Ref*. ix. 13 ff.) for the reverencing of the elements.

[2] Percy, *Probleme*, pp. 177 f., for instance, points out that the distinction between the powers of the lower world and the higher world opened by the Saviour is more at home in St Paul's own theology than that of his opponents; and, again, that the evidence is against the Colossians

What may be said is that the error was sufficiently grave, at all events, for St Paul, for his part, to describe an adherent of it as detached from Christ (ii. 19, οὐ κρατῶν τὴν κεφαλήν).[1] It is noteworthy, however, that he does not meet these errors with mere denunciation. He 'can be as vehement and outspoken as anyone..., but he knows also how to appeal to the reason and the understanding..., and, above all, how to correct erroneous views by a constant emphasis on his readers' experience of God in Christ'. Such was Dr Vincent Taylor's estimate of St Paul's methods, in contrast with the denunciations in II Peter and Jude; and he continued: 'This is especially evident in Colossians and Ephesians, where, as Professor E. F. Scott has reminded us, his argument is essentially religious, and is of permanent value because it rests on a sure conviction of the pre-eminence of Christ and the absolute value of the Christian faith.'[2]

APPENDIX TO P. 19 ABOVE

A striking comment on the situation is provided by the following notice relating to two slaves who had run away. The document (*Pap. Par.* 10) is adduced by Dibelius in his commentary on Philemon; but the text given below is from U. Wilcken, *Urkunden der Ptolemäerzeit*, I, no. 121, pp. 566 ff., and the translation and notes are based on his, although

making a sharp antithesis between the Law and the Saviour, as later Gnostics did, and as, in a sense, St Paul did. See also a cautious statement by Bo Reicke in *J.N.T.S.* I, no. 2 (Nov. 1954), pp. 137 ff., as to the degree to which the Dead Sea sect might be likened to Gnostics. Also the valuable article by K. G. Kuhn, 'Die in Palästina gefundenen hebräischen Texte und das Neue Testament', in *Z.T.K.* XLVII (1950), pp. 193 ff.

[1] Mr Fenton Morley, in the work referred to on p. 30, n. 1, puts forward the view that, in fact, it was not a party but an individual who was doing the damage; and that the person was outside the Christian church. But I think it is difficult to build on the singular, when it is the indefinite τις.

[2] V. Taylor in *E.T.* XLV (1933–4), 439 (citing E. F. Scott, *Moffatt Commentary* on Colossians, Philemon, and Ephesians, pp. 10 ff.).

justice cannot here be done to his carefully documented and qualified suggestions. I owe thanks to Dr A. H. McDonald of Clare College for help in compiling this note.

Τοῦ κε Ἐπεὶφ ις. Ἀριστογένου τοῦ Χρυσίππου | Ἀλαβανδέως πρεσβευτοῦ παῖς ἀνακεχώ|ρηκεν (2) ἐν Ἀλεξανδρείαι, (1) ὧι ὄνομα Ἕρμων, ὃς καὶ Νεῖλος | καλεῖται, τὸ γένος Σύρος ἀπὸ Βαμβύκης, | ὡς ἐτῶν ιη, μεγέθει μέσος, ἀγένειος | εὔκνημος κοιλογένειος, φακὸς παρὰ ῥῖνα | ἐξ ἀριστερῶν, οὐλὴ ὑπὲρ χαλινὸν ἐξ ἀριστερῶν, | ἐστιγμένος τὸν δεξιὸν καρπὸν γράμμασι | βαρβαρικοῖς δυσίν, ἔχων χρυσίου ἐπισήμου | μναιεῖα γ, πῖνας ι, κρίκκον σιδηροῦν, | ἐν ὧι λήκυθος καὶ ξύστραι, καὶ περὶ τὸ σῶμα | χλαμύδα καὶ περίζωμα. Τοῦτον ὃς ἂν ἀνα|γάγῃ, λήψεται χαλκοῦ β (2) γ, (1) ἐφ᾿ ἱεροῦ δείξας α (2) β | (1) παρ᾿ ἀνδρὶ ἀξιοχρείωι καὶ δωσιδίκωι γ (2) ε. | (1) Μηνύειν δὲ τὸν βουλόμενον τοῖς παρὰ τοῦ | στρατηγοῦ. ‖ Ἔστιν δὲ καὶ ὁ συναποδεδρακὼς αὐτῶι | Βίων δοῦλος Καλλικράτου τῶν περὶ αὐλὴν | ἀρχυπηρετῶν, μεγέθει βραχύς, πλατὺς | ἀπὸ τῶν ὤμων, κατάκνημος, χαροπός, | ὃς καὶ ἔχων ἀνακεχώρηκεν ἱμάτιον καὶ | ἱματίδιον παιδαρίου καὶ σεβίτιον γυναι|κεῖον ἄξιον ς καὶ χαλκοῦ * * Ἐ. | τοῦτον ὃς ἂν ἀναγ⟨άγ⟩ῃ λήψεται ὅσα καὶ ὑπὲρ τοῦ | προγεγραμμένου. Μηνύειν δὲ καὶ ὑπὲρ | τούτου τοῖς παρὰ τοῦ στρατηγοῦ.

The figure (2) in the text indicates additions by a second hand, and (1) the return to the first hand. It is not known where the document was found, but it may belong to Memphis. In any case, it is evidently a copy of the original placard at Alexandria (that is why, outside Alexandria, the second hand needed to add 'at Alexandria'); and the rewards for returning the slaves were raised (see the second hand) as time went on, or as the search went further afield. One or two letters are uncertain, but this is not indicated in the present transcript. The date (the 25th year, the 16th of the month Epeiph) is believed by Wilcken to represent 13 August 156 B.C. (under Ptolemy Philometor): the alternative is 145 B.C.

TRANSLATION

The 25th (year), Epeiph 16. The servant of Aristogenes the son of Chrysippus, an ambassador of Alabanda, has run away [at Alexandria]. Name, Hermon, *alias* Nilus. Nationality, Syrian, of Bambyke (i.e. Hierapolis). Age, about 18, of medium height, clean-shaven, sturdy in the leg, with a dimple in the chin, a mole on the left of the nose, a scar above the left corner of the mouth, tattooed (or branded?) on the right wrist with two foreign characters (possibly, suggests Wilcken, the Aramaic initials of the deities Hadad and 'Atargatis). He has 3 *mnaieia* (gold coins) of coined gold, 10 pearls, an iron ring on which are a flask and scrapers (i.e. possibly a neck-ring engraved with these objects, indicating that Hermon was a bath-slave). He is wearing a cloak and an undergarment. Anybody bringing him back (i.e. in person) will receive 2 [3] (talents) in bronze; (anybody doing so) by indicating that he is (in asylum) at a temple, 1 [2] (talent(s)); (anybody doing so by indicating that he is) with a substantial person who is subject to the law, 3 [5] (talents). And anybody wishing to give information may do so to the governor's representatives.

There is also one Bion, the slave of Callicrates, one of the chief officers at court (possibly an officer in the royal garrison?), who has run away with him: short, broad-shouldered, thin (or, possibly, sturdy, like εὐκν. above) in the leg, with blue-grey(?) eyes. He also has run away with a coat and a slave's small coat and a woman's box (? a sort of 'vanity bag') worth 6 talents and 5** (?5000 copper drachmas may have been meant. The text is defective). Anybody returning him will receive the same as for the aforesaid. Information may be given about him also to the governor's representatives.

NOTE. The chief problem in this document is the meaning of the actions for which the various rewards are offered.

This translation assumes that ὅς ἂν ἀναγάγῃ means bringing back in person, while the phrases which follow refer to compassing his restoration by informing. It appears that by no means all temples possessed rights of asylum. But in any case, asylum only ensured proper enquiry, not absolute protection. Reward for information leading to recovery of the slave by this duly authorized process would be less than that for information that the slave was with a private person; for a private person was liable to pay a penalty for harbouring a runaway, and the reward for information could afford to be correspondingly higher.

III. TEXTUAL CRITICISM OF THE PAULINE EPISTLES[1]

Since exegesis must go hand-in-hand with textual criticism, the student of the interpretation of the New Testament needs to have some acquaintance with both the materials for the establishment of the text of the New Testament, and the principles governing their use for that purpose. The present note is designed as an introduction to the subject for beginners in the art of textual criticism, so far as it is concerned with the Pauline Epistles. A good popular account is contained in *Our Bible and the Ancient Manuscripts* by Sir Frederic Kenyon (4th ed., 1939): for more advanced study the same author's *The Textual Criticism of the New Testament* (Macmillan) may be recommended, and A. H. McNeill and C. S. C. Williams' *Introduction to the N.T.* (Oxford, 1953); and, for a full discussion of the textual criticism of the Pauline Epistles, *The Text of the Epistles* by G. Zuntz (*Schweich Lectures* for 1946, Oxford University Press).

[1] This section is kindly contributed by the Rev. J. N. Sanders, Dean of Peterhouse.

I. MATERIALS

The materials for the establishment of the text of the Pauline Epistles consist of (*a*) Greek manuscripts; (*b*) ancient translations; (*c*) quotations in the writings of early Christian authors.

(*a*) Manuscripts are either on papyrus or vellum. Of the papyri, the most important is p[46] (the Chester Beatty Papyrus), which was written about A.D. 200, and contains (with some omissions due to imperfections in the papyrus, chiefly in Romans and I Thessalonians) Romans, Hebrews, I and II Corinthians, Ephesians, Galatians, Philippians, Colossians, I Thessalonians in that order. It is a codex (a single pile of leaves folded like a modern exercise book), and the missing portion probably contained II Thessalonians. How much else (if anything) it had cannot be ascertained. There cannot have been room for all the remaining Pauline Epistles.

Of vellum manuscripts, some are written in uncials (separate capitals), others in minuscules (small letters, which could be written continuously).

The most important uncials are:

א Codex Sinaiticus, of the fourth century;

A Codex Alexandrinus, of the fifth century;

B Codex Vaticanus, of the fourth century, lacking the Pastoral Epistles and most of Hebrews; and

C Codex Ephraemi Rescriptus, of the fifth century, which was later broken up and reused for a Syriac text, but of which there still remain readable substantial parts of all the Pauline Epistles except II Thessalonians.

These were originally all manuscripts of the whole Bible. In addition, three uncial manuscripts of the Epistles may be mentioned:

D_2 Codex Claromontanus, of the sixth century, which contains a Latin translation facing the Greek;

G₃ Codex Boernerianus, of the ninth century, with an interlinear Latin translation; and

H₃ Codex Euthalianus, of the sixth century, consisting of a few fragments only, and containing the text of an edition made at Caesarea some time in the fourth century and attributed to Euthalius.

Three minuscules are particularly important:

33, of the ninth or tenth century;

424, of the tenth century, but containing marginal readings (denoted by 424**) from an ancient uncial; and

1739, of the tenth century, with a type of text closely resembling that known to Origen.

(*b*) Of the ancient translations, the most important are the Latin, Egyptian, and Syriac.

There are two forms of the Latin version, the 'Old Latin' made before the time of St Jerome, and St Jerome's Vulgate. Examples of the Old Latin are the Latin texts in D₂ and G₃, and fragments of a sixth-century manuscript of the Pauline Epistles known by the symbol r.

The Egyptian translations are in the two chief Coptic dialects, Sahidic and Bohairic. Both versions were made probably in the third century, the Sahidic being the earlier of the two.

No trace exists of any 'Old Syriac' version of the Pauline Epistles: the earliest version is the *Peshitta*, the Syriac equivalent of the Latin Vulgate, probably made late in the fourth or early in the fifth century. In 616 the *Peshitta* was revised by Thomas of Harkel, with the aid of ancient Greek manuscripts at Alexandria, and his version is known as the *Harklean*. It contains some interesting variant readings, both Syriac and Greek.

(*c*) Quotations of Scripture in early ecclesiastical writers are important as enabling us to identify the type of text current in a particular church at a particular time, often much earlier than our earliest manuscripts. Particularly important are Marcion, Tertullian, and Origen.

2. PRINCIPLES

The collected edition of St Paul's Epistles was probably made not later than A.D. 100, but, even so, an interval of some forty years elapsed between the actual writing of the Epistles and their collection. Another century intervenes between the collection of the Epistles and our earliest manuscript, p[46], and a still longer period between it and the earliest vellum manuscripts. It was upon the latter, chiefly ℵ and B, that Westcott and Hort relied in the main in compiling their justly celebrated text of the New Testament, published in 1881. During the whole period of manuscript tradition errors gradually accumulated, and it is the task of the critic to eliminate these, as far as he may. The introduction to Westcott and Hort's edition gives a classic formulation of the principles that should guide the textual critic in his task, and their principles may still be applied, though their results require modification, if only because of the fresh material that has come to light since their time. Of this p[46] is the outstanding example.

Briefly, their principles are that where manuscripts have different readings, the supporters of the variants must not simply be counted, but weighed and classified. They must be weighed according to the relative probability of the readings they contain, and that probability is of two kinds, 'intrinsic' and 'transcriptional'. Intrinsic probability is by itself untrustworthy, since it depends on the individual critic's subjective judgement that one reading is preferable to, and so more probable than, another. It must therefore be reinforced, or modified, by considering transcriptional probability, i.e. by considering which reading best accounts for the existing variants. It is, for example, transcriptional probability which led Westcott and Hort to prefer a shorter to a longer reading, on the assumption that copyists are more likely to have inserted glosses, or paraphrased obscure passages, than to have made omissions from the text of Scripture.

Applying these principles, Westcott and Hort distinguished between the mass of later manuscripts (which they called 'Syrian') and two smaller groups of manuscripts, on the whole much earlier in date, which shared certain characteristics distinct from each other and from the 'Syrian' manuscripts, and which they called 'Neutral' and 'Western' respectively. The 'Syrian' text is found in the majority of minuscules, and in some later uncials, and, in an early form, in the *Peshitta*. The 'Neutral' text, which they so named because they believed it substantially free from corruption, they found in ℵ and B, as well as in A (in the Pauline Epistles, though not in the Gospels) and C, in the minuscules 33 and 424**, and in the Egyptian versions. Their 'Western' text, so called because they believed it to have originated in the West, is chiefly represented (in the Pauline Epistles) by D_2 and G_3, the Old Latin, and the variant readings noted in the Harklean Syriac. They regarded it as ancient, but corrupt in comparison with the Neutral.

Subsequent study, and discoveries of fresh evidence, have led to the realization that both 'Neutral' and 'Western' are misnomers. The 'Neutral' appears to have been the result of deliberate emendation by scholars whose conception of 'intrinsic probability' resembled Westcott and Hort's: it is an Egyptian text, and not the first that existed in Egypt. It is noteworthy that p^{46} exhibits a type of text unlike both the 'Neutral' and the 'Western'. Also the Western text was far more extensively used in ancient times than Westcott and Hort realized. It is rather a group of texts more ancient than the revisions that produced the 'Neutral' and 'Syrian' texts, and attested from many parts of the ancient Christian world, including Egypt. It has also come to be realized that the 'Syrian' text may contain genuinely ancient readings—for instance, p^{46} contains a few readings otherwise attested only by 'Syrian' authorities! The non-'Neutral', non-'Syrian' texts are by no means homogeneous. Some are geographically Western, like the African Old Latin; others were associated with other ancient churches. In particular, a group of Gospel manuscripts has been isolated which is believed to represent the text current in the church of Caesarea. It has not so far proved possible to identify the Caesarean text of the Pauline Epistles, though H_3 and 1739 may be examples of it.

Exclusive reliance on the 'Neutral' text, or on any single form of text, is no longer possible. When the authorities have been classified, on whatever principle, the necessity of informed and responsible choice between these readings still lies upon the critic.

NOTES

THE EPISTLE TO THE COLOSSIANS

i. 1, 2. *Greetings from Paul and Timothy to the Christians at Colossae.* See A Note on Christian Greetings in Letters, p. 153.

1. ἀπόστολος. See A Note on Ἀπόστολος, p. 155.

διὰ θελήματος Θεοῦ probably qualifies ἀπόστολος Χ. Ἰ.: it was by God's will that this vocation came.

ἀδελφός is a common term in the N.T. for 'a Christian' (see next note and Philem. 16): 'our brother T.'

2. τοῖς ἐν Κολοσσαῖς ἁγίοις καὶ πιστοῖς ἀδελφοῖς ἐν Χριστῷ. ἅγιος is perhaps best rendered 'dedicated', 'God's own', because it represents the O.T. conception of 'the dedicated people' whose members are 'the dedicated ones'. In Hebrew the root QDŠ (קדשׁ) is the most important in this connexion, connoting separation. 'Saint' is, to modern ears, misleading, for the Hebrew and Greek words are concerned less with any excellence of character (however much that may be implied as a *result*) than with the commitments and loyalties of the Church to the God who has made her his own. See on iii. 12 below. πιστός, accordingly, comes very near to the same sense, and helps to clinch and strengthen the idea of Christians as the real Israel: they are *a brotherhood dedicated and loyal to God.*

This interpretation assumes that ἁγίοις καὶ πιστοῖς is to be taken as part of the description of the ἀδελφοί. To treat τοῖς ἁγίοις as a noun—'the members of God's people'—and the rest as descriptive, would probably require the repetition of the article: τοῖς καὶ πιστοῖς κ.τ.λ.

There is ample evidence that St Paul employed this famous formula, ἐν Χριστῷ, ἐν Κυρίῳ, etc., to describe Christians as 'incorporated' in Christ, united with him as closely as limbs are united with the body to which they belong. It does not follow that he intends this every time he uses the preposition ἐν with Χριστός, Κύριος, etc.: sometimes it is an instrumental use, sometimes it has other shades of meaning. But here it does appear to be correct to take it as 'incorporative'. Note that St Paul (unlike the Fourth Evangelist) avoids speaking of Christ as 'in God'. Even Col. iii. 3 stops short of saying so explicitly. See notes there.

The alternative—namely, to take ἐν X. as dependent on πιστοῖς (='who trust in Christ')—is most improbable, for (a) it is not easy, as has been said, to separate ἁγίοις (taking it as a noun, 'dedicated persons') from πιστοῖς ἀδελφοῖς, especially when there is only one definite article; (b) if πιστοῖς 'governed' ἐν X. it would more naturally *follow* ἀδελφοῖς; and in any case, (c) πιστοῖς ἐν as='trusting in' cannot be paralleled in the N.T. except (at most, and doubtfully) by Eph. i. 1.[1] Finally, (d) the omission of the definite article τοῖς before ἐν X. is a not unknown phenomenon in N.T. Greek: see (besides the πίστις passages in the footnote) Phil. i. 14 (τῶν ἀδελφῶν ἐν K. probably = ...τῶν ἐν K.); Eph. i. 1 (where, for all the textual uncertainty, the same construction as is used here may be intended); Mark vi. 6 (perhaps); Luke iv. 20, 28; and, below, Col. i. 8 τὴν ὑμῶν ἀγάπην ἐν Πνεύματι.

ἀπὸ Θεοῦ Πατρὸς ἡμῶν. This is the only one of the Pauline epistles in which Christ is not coupled with God in the greetings formula (and in inferior texts scribes have made up the deficiency). It is difficult to divine any reason for the omission. In any case, the apostle proceeds immediately to a description of Christ in more exalted terms than in any of his other epistles.

[1] The *verb*, πιστεύω, is rarely enough used with ἐν (in the N.T. at most only in Mark i. 15 and perhaps John iii. 15, *si vera lectio*); the *noun*, πίστις, is used with ἐν in i. 4 below, in Eph. i. 15, I Tim. iii. 13, II Tim. iii. 15, and possibly Rom. iii. 25; but in all these passages it is doubtful whether ἐν indicates the *object* of faith so much as its *sphere*. See on i. 4 below, and contrast the unambiguous phrase in ii. 5, ...τῆς εἰς Χριστὸν πίστεως ὑμῶν. In Eph. iii. 12 ἐν ᾧ is clearly 'incorporative', and πίστις is there followed by a *genitive* of the object.

46

i. 3–14. *A fervent thanksgiving for the reliance upon God and the love which the Christians at Colossae have shown, and for the work of God through Christ from which this springs; and an account of the apostle's constant prayer for these friends whom he has never met.*

An expression of thanksgiving occurs immediately after the greeting in every extant Pauline Epistle except Galatians and (if they be Pauline) I Timothy and Titus. In II Cor. i. 3, instead of εὐχαριστεῖν, the fervent εὐλογητὸς ὁ Θεός is used.

It is immensely valuable for anybody who desires to learn how to pray to take careful note of the substance of the great prayer indicated in these verses, and of its structure, and of its parallels elsewhere. Its substance and shape may be roughly shown thus:

(i) the actual *petition* is for—

(*v.* 9)   a sensitiveness to God's will consisting in a grasp of what is spiritually valuable,

(*v.* 10) issuing in conduct worthy of Christians, and pleasing to Christ—namely, in a crop of good activities and a growth in understanding;

(*v.* 11) the equipment for this being strength, a strength derived from God's power (a power which is in keeping with his revealed splendour), a strength which cheerfully stays the course.

(ii) Then comes *thanksgiving*—

(*vv.* 12–14) for light, for love, for rescue from evil.

But (iii) the prayer had already sprung out of an *antecedent* thanksgiving: its foundation is the solid fact of what God has done (alluded to already in *vv.* 5–7), and to this it returns in *vv.* 12–14.

Observe that the actual petition is chiefly for *discernment* of God's will and the *power* to perform it (Phil. i. 9–11 presents an interesting parallel). These themes return in ii. 1–5; and cf. iv. 12.

As for parallels to the theme and structure, almost every book of the N.T. provides them (not to mention parts of the O.T. also, though with obvious limitations); and it is noteworthy that the solid fact of what God has done is always the 'perch' (so to speak) from which Christian prayer takes its flight and to which it returns.

A study of the 'shape' of Christian prayer is to be found in Dr M. A. C. Warren's *Together with God* (Church Missionary Society, London; foreword dated 1947), which strikingly demonstrates its general uniformity: 'after this manner pray ye' was evidently a carefully observed injunction.

3. Εὐχαριστοῦμεν. Is this an 'epistolary' plural, = 'I thank', or a real plural, = 'Timothy and I thank'? In favour of the latter is the singular in *vv.* 23, 24 (where St Paul is speaking exclusively of himself). But it is a nicely balanced issue; consider, e.g., the singulars and plurals in I Thess. ii and iii. See Karl Dick, *Der schriftstellerische Plural bei Paulus* (Halle, 1900) and Roller, *Formular*, pp. 169ff. Roller is, broadly speaking, in favour of taking the plurals literally; and Lightfoot (on Col. iv. 3) declares that 'there is no reason to think that St Paul ever uses an "epistolary" plural referring to himself solely'. So W. F. Lofthouse in *E.T* LVIII, no. 7 (April 1947), pp. 179ff. and LXIV, no. 8 (May 1953), pp. 241ff.

τῷ Θεῷ Πατρὶ τοῦ Κυρίου ἡμῶν.... This is by no means certainly the correct reading (B 1739 sy, as against τῷ Θ. τῷ Π. D* G Chr, or τῷ Θ. καὶ Π. ℵ A I *pl* ς). But it is so unusual that it is arguable that it is the original, of which the variants are modifications. Note: (i) its ambiguity. Does it mean 'to God, who is the Father of our Lord...' (as though it were τῷ Θ. τῷ), or 'to him who is both God and the Father of our Lord...' (as though τῷ Θ. καὶ Π.)? (ii) Its rarity. Only here and in ii. 2, iii. 17 (if there too this reading be adopted) and in *v.* 12 below (if this reading—

which has less support in that verse—were to be adopted there also) does this particular phrase, ὁ Θεὸς Πατήρ, occur (with one definite article and without καί). Elsewhere it is Θεὸς Πατήρ or Θεὸς καὶ Πατήρ or ὁ Θεὸς καὶ Πατήρ or ὁ Θεὸς ὁ Πατήρ. It is to be noticed that, in these phrases, καί is more often used with the nominative than when the phrase is in the oblique cases. See Burton, *Galatians*, pp. 384 ff., for a careful examination of Πατήρ as applied to God.

The translation 'God, who is the Father...' seems best.

πάντοτε. This, as a comparison of the epistolary formulae shows, is to be taken with εὐχαριστοῦμεν ('we always give thanks about you when we pray'). See Schubert, 'Form and Function', especially p. 66. (But note that, unusually, he takes Phil. i. 3 ἐπὶ πάσῃ τῇ μνείᾳ ὑμῶν to mean, not 'whenever I think of you', but 'for every expression of your remembrance of me'; see pp. 74 ff.)

4. τὴν πίστιν ὑμῶν ἐν X. 'I. The ἐν probably indicates the sphere rather than the object of the faith; cf. on *v.* 2 above. For the whole verse, there is a close parallel in Philem. 5.

5. διὰ τὴν ἐλπίδα κ.τ.λ. To what part of the sentence does this phrase belong? Is the hope the ground of the thanksgiving (*v.* 3) or of the faith and love (*v.* 4)? The latter seems the more likely, because both faith and love are closer to it in position, and because the ground of the thanksgiving has already been defined in the clause ἀκούσαντες κ.τ.λ.

If so, it is remarkable that trust and love are described as dependent on ἐλπίς—the goal of Christian expectation: so remarkable, that alternative explanations are sometimes offered. Yet it seems possible; for ἡ ἐλπίς, the Christian confidence that, in Christ, God's way of love 'has the last word', is not only future: already it is the source of steadiness and of active concern for fellow-Christians. 'Hope', in this distinctively Christian sense, is anything but a mere 'opiate of the people' or a mere prize 'in the sky' reserved only for the future. Precisely because it is stored in heaven (ἀποκειμένην . . . ἐν τοῖς οὐρανοῖς), it is a potent incentive to action here and now.

Almost unawares, St Paul has repeated the classic triad of I Cor. xiii, πίστις, ἐλπίς, ἀγάπη; cf. I Thess. i. 3.

προηκούσατε: I.e. probably, 'heard before the false teaching', rather than 'before the time of writing' or 'before a future fulfilment'. So, too, the phrases which follow, in *vv.* 6f., may well be chosen by way of contrast with the false teaching: the Gospel is true, universal, and concerned not with decrees of men's devising but with the graciousness of God. In Eph. i. 12, on the other hand, τοὺς προηλπικότας ἐν τῷ Χριστῷ appears to refer to the priority of Jews over Gentiles.

ἐν τῷ λόγῳ τῆς ἀληθείας τοῦ εὐαγγελίου: I.e. 'when the true Gospel—the Gospel as it really is—was spoken to you' (cf. *v.* 6 below); or, alternatively, the ἐν may be instrumental, of the means by which they heard of the hope. Masson takes τοῦ εὐαγγελίου as in apposition to τῆς ἀληθείας—'the truth, that is, the Gospel'. This seems less probable, but in any case the meaning is scarcely affected.

6. καρποφορούμενον καὶ αὐξανόμενον. The middle, καρποφορεῖσθαι, is found elsewhere only in an inscription (see Bauer, *s.v.*): contrast the active in *v.* 10. But it is difficult (*pace* Lightfoot and others) to believe that any difference in sense is intended. Applied here to the Gospel, the words are applied in *v.* 10 to the Colossian Christians themselves. (Note that in Gen. i. 22 etc., where the Hebrew, 'Be fruitful and multiply', might have been rendered by these words, the LXX does *not* use καρποφορεῖν.) The words are reminiscent, a little, of John xv. 1 ff., and, far more, of the Parable of the Sower in the Marcan form (Mark iv. 8), where the seed in good soil ἐδίδου καρπὸν ἀναβαίνοντα καὶ αὐξανόμενα (αὐξάνεσθαι is absent from the parallels in Matthew and Luke). And incidentally, the application of the words both to the Gospel and to its recipients is itself reminiscent of the

interpretation of the parable in Mark iv. 14 ff. In both
Mark and this epistle, also, fruit-bearing is mentioned, sur-
prisingly, *before* the growth (as again in *v.* 10 below). But
how far St Paul's words are actually derived from the
Gospel traditions it is impossible to say. W. L. Knox,
Gentiles, p. 149, n. 5, besides discussing this question, maintains that 'the phrase is a regular Gnostic catchword', and
suggests that St Paul has borrowed the favourite phrases of
the teaching which he was attacking, to turn them against
the false teachers: *they* said (perhaps) that there was much
fruit-bearing and growth needed beyond the stage of mere
faith in Christ; *Paul* avers that faith in Christ is itself the
seed, alive and growing. Moreover, it is universally
attested (ἐν παντὶ τῷ κόσμῳ).

As for the distinct meanings of the two words, Chrysostom's comment is that 'fruit-bearing' means a crop of good
deeds (cf. Phil. i. 11), and 'the growth of the Gospel' refers
to the growing number of converts (καρποφορούμενον διὰ
τὰ ἔργα, αὐξανόμενον τῷ πολλοὺς παραλαμβάνειν κ.τ.λ.,
quoted by Dibelius *in loc.*). If so, αὐξάνεσθαι must be given
a slightly different turn in *v.* 10, as is indeed shown by the
addition of τῇ ἐπιγνώσει τοῦ Θεοῦ—unless that is instrumental, meaning not *in* but *by* the knowledge of God: so
Lohmeyer, etc. In Rom. i. 13 (ἵνα τινὰ καρπὸν σχῶ καὶ ἐν
ὑμῖν...) καρπός appears to refer to the results of evangelism.

ἐν ἀληθείᾳ: I.e. the grace of God 'as it truly is', 'un-
travestied' (cf. *v.* 5 above). Alternatively, it is possible,
though less likely, that ἀλήθεια virtually = 'the Gospel' (so
Dibelius, citing II Cor. iv. 2, vi. 7, Gal. ii. 14, v. 7;
and cf. Masson on *v.* 5 above): it would then be a virtual
repetition of ἐν τῷ λόγῳ κ.τ.λ. above.

7. συνδούλου: 'A slave, like St Paul, of Christ'. See on
συναιχμάλωτος, iv. 10 below.

ὑπὲρ ὑμῶν. Read, rather, ἡμῶν. See Introduction,
p. 27, n. 1.

8. ἐν Πνεύματι. The word πνεῦμα is a problem to translators. The absence of the definite article does not necessarily mean that the Holy Spirit is not intended: the phrase *could* mean 'your love which is engendered in the sphere of the Holy Spirit' (cf. Rom. xiv. 17 δικαιοσύνη καὶ εἰρήνη καὶ χαρὰ ἐν Πνεύματι Ἁγίῳ). But here the sense may well be something more general—'your more than merely human love', 'your spiritual, supernaturally derived love'; cf. the adjective πνευματικῇ in *v.* 9. There is practically nothing in this epistle about the Holy Spirit; although others (e.g. Romans) are rich in allusions.

9. Διὰ τοῦτο καὶ.... The καί is apparently to be regarded as belonging to the διὰ τοῦτο rather than to the ἡμεῖς: 'that is *precisely* why', or 'that, in fact, is why...'. To link it with the pronoun ('that is why *we* also...') does not seem to be appropriate here; and there are other passages also where, even when the καί is fused (by 'crasis') with ἐγώ (διὰ τοῦτο κἀγὼ...), the context demands that it be dissociated from the ἐγώ. See I Thess. ii. 13, iii. 5, Rom. iii. 7, Eph. i. 15.

ἵνα πληρωθῆτε τὴν ἐπίγνωσιν.... Cf. Phil. i. 11 πεπληρωμένοι καρπὸν δικαιοσύνης. Masson holds that this means not 'that you may be filled *with* the knowledge...' (or 'crop' in Philippians), but 'that you may come to maturity *in respect of* the knowledge...' (similarly in Philippians). He argues that ἐπίγνωσις is not a measurable commodity but a process. It is certainly true (i) that the interpretation of *v.* 10 αὐξανόμενοι τῇ ἐπιγνώσει τοῦ Θεοῦ *can* be squared with this; and (ii) that πληρόω with an accusative of content is *rare*. But this latter construction is not *unknown*: Acts ii. 28 πληρώσεις με εὐφροσύνην (even if this is an inferior reading to εὐφροσύνης) suggests that a scribe thought it possible; Ex. xxxi. 3 ἐνέπλησα αὐτὸν πνεῦμα...σοφίας is relevant; and so is the comparable γέμειν with acc. in Rev. xvii. 3 (see D.-B. § 159 *Anh.*, Abel § 43 j *rem.* for references), and the phrase in *v.* 10 is, I think, equally capable of being squared with this.

Moreover, Rom. xv. 14, πεπληρωμένοι πάσης τῆς γνώσεως, although this is the common construction (with gen.), shows that 'to be filled with γνῶσις' is a Pauline conception. Fortunately, the general sense is not greatly affected by the choice between the alternatives.

τὴν ἐπίγνωσιν τοῦ θελήματος αὐτοῦ. See A Note on the Knowledge of God, p. 159. Here it may be said summarily (cf. Dibelius as cited there):

(i) (ἡ) ἐπίγνωσις τῆς ἀληθείας eventually became one of the regular terms for 'Christianity', as contrasted with false and erroneous systems; but

(ii) behind this and kindred phrases (which by themselves might sound as though they referred only to an intellectual process, of the mind and not necessarily of the will and affections) there lay the rich material of the experience of a personal God revealed in Jesus Christ. They did not mean merely a mental grasp of abstract propositions; they meant 'the perception of God's will as seen in Christ, and the response to it (or rather, to *him*)'—'the entering into that divulged secret (μυστήριον) which is Christ'—carrying all the implications of a changed life and conduct (see especially the context of the present passage); in short,

(iii) our 'knowledge of God' in this sense is dependent upon our *being known by God*—I Cor. xiii. 12, Gal. iv. 9— and is in sharp contrast to the ψευδώνυμος γνῶσις, the 'knowledge falsely so called', of I Tim. vi. 20.

The best comment on the whole conception is, perhaps, Matt. xi. 25–7, Luke x. 21 f. (Christ's expression of reciprocal knowledge between the Father and himself).

ἐν πάσῃ σοφίᾳ καὶ συνέσει πνευματικῇ seems to define the preceding phrase: perception of God's will consists in wisdom and understanding of every sort, on the spiritual level. Contrast I Cor. i. 20, etc. It is perhaps significant that the parable of the sower, already cited on *v.* 6 above, contains (this time in its Matthean form) the phrase ἀκούων καὶ συνιείς, Matt. xiii. 23, and the passage from Isa. vi cited in the same context, Matt. xiii. 15 etc., has μή ποτε... συνῶσιν.

10. εἰς πᾶσαν ἀρεσκείαν. ἀρέσκειν, ἀρεσκεία with a *human* object tends to represent a *bad* quality ('complaisance', 'obsequiousness', 'cringing'—L. and S. citing Aristotle and Theophrastus): see iii. 22 below, Gal. i. 10, I Thess. ii. 4. But as directed towards *God*, it represents the religious ideal: II Cor. v. 9 φιλοτιμούμεθα, εἴτε ἐνδημοῦντες εἴτε ἐκδημοῦντες, εὐάρεστοι αὐτῷ εἶναι. So in iii. 20 below, and in the LXX.

ἐν παντὶ ἔργῳ ἀγαθῷ κ.τ.λ. If the interpretation mentioned in the note on *v.* 6 above is right, this phrase provides a striking instance of the verbal arrangement (*a b b a*) called 'chiasmus':

(A) noun: ἐν παντὶ ἔργῳ ἀγαθῷ ⟍ (B) verb: καρποφοροῦντες
(B) verb: αὐξανόμενοι   ⟋ (A) noun: τῇ ἐπιγνώσει
                                                     τοῦ Θεοῦ

Cf. on Philem. 5. But alternatively, if τῇ ἐπιγνώσει is instrumental, καρποφ. and αὐξαν. must be taken together, and with both ἐν παντὶ ἔργῳ ἀγαθῷ and τῇ ἐπιγνώσει: 'yielding fruit and growing in every good deed by means of the knowledge of God'.

11. κατὰ τὸ κράτος τῆς δόξης αὐτοῦ: I.e. (perhaps) 'in virtue of the power which belongs to God as he has revealed himself to men'—for that is especially what 'glory' in the Bible implies. See note on Glory below, after i. 27.

εἰς πᾶσαν ὑπομονὴν καὶ μακροθυμίαν. Lightfoot notes that, broadly speaking (though there are exceptions), ὑπομονή may be called the opposite of *cowardice* and *despondency* and is allied to *hope*, while μακροθυμία may be contrasted with *wrath* and *revenge* and coupled with *mercy*.

The εἰς denotes the issue of the process described in the preceding sentences: 'leading to...'.

μετὰ χαρᾶς. 'Joy' and related words are strikingly close, in the Christian vocabulary, to circumstances calling for both ὑπομονή and μακροθυμία, e.g. Matt. v. 12, Acts v. 41, James i. 2 f., I Pet. iv. 13. If χαρά is not rooted in the soil of suffering, it is shallow, Matt. xiii. 20 f. Thus, it seems better to connect this with what precedes than with the following εὐχαριστοῦντες, despite the punctuation of editors.

12. εὐχαριστοῦντες is more naturally construed with the preceding participles and with reference to the Colossians, than with οὐ παυόμεθα in v. 9, as though it referred to the apostle; and that, even if we read ἡμᾶς, not ὑμᾶς, for it would be quite natural for St Paul at this point to include himself with his friends.

τῷ Πατρί. Except in the Fourth Gospel and the Johannine epistles, '(the) Father' (without the addition of 'God' or of a qualifying genitive or possessive) is not common in the N.T. It occurs in the vocative (or nominative used as vocative) in Matt. xi. 26, Luke x. 21, xi. 2, xxii. 42, xxiii. 34, 46, and ('Αββᾶ ὁ Πατήρ) in Mark xiv. 36, Rom. viii. 15, Gal. iv. 6. Otherwise, only here and Matt. xi. 27 (‖ Luke x. 22), xxiv. 36 (‖ Mark xiii. 32), xxviii. 19, Luke ix. 26, Acts i. 4, 7, ii. 33, Rom. vi. 4, Eph. ii. 18, iii. 14.

The addition or substitution of (τῷ) Θεῷ in certain MSS. is opposed by a weighty and representative group (p⁴⁶ ABD *pc* vgʷ *s*), and is evidently a scribal alteration.

τῷ ἱκανώσαντι κ.τ.λ.: 'Who has qualified you (see textual note, Introduction, p. 27, n. 1) to take your share in the territory allotted to God's people—that realm of light'. This is a pictorial phrase, built in part round the O.T. picture of the educative process by which God trained and qualified the chosen people to enter the promised land which he had assigned to them as their portion. So with Christians, who are 'the Israel of God', God's glorious power is able to 'qualify' them (inherently unworthy though they are) to enter that spiritual land of promise, that realm of

light. See further on iii. 24 below. But although the verb
ἱκανόω occurs also in II Cor. iii. 6, it is not, in its LXX
occurrences, associated with the idea of 'qualifying' Israel
for their destiny.

13, 14. ὃς ἐρρύσατο κ.τ.λ. This famous clause is charged
with ideas of great importance and of wide range. Some of
these are here noted.

(i) In *v.* 14, ἔχομεν appears to be the correct reading, as
against ἔσχομεν. (The latter is read by B (alone of MSS.)
and is represented by the Bohairic and Arabic versions and
by quotations in Jerome. It also appears as a variant in the
parallel passage Eph. i. 7; see Lightfoot, p. 251.) If so,
there is a significant contrast between this present tense and
the aorists which precede it: ἔχομεν represents the continued result of the rescue effected in the past.

(ii) A very striking parallel to the whole phrase is provided by Acts xxvi. 18, where Paul, before Agrippa, is
represented as saying that, in the commission given to him
by the risen Christ on the Damascus road, came the words
ἀνοῖξαι ὀφθαλμοὺς αὐτῶν, τοῦ ἐπιστρέψαι ἀπὸ σκότους εἰς φῶς
καὶ τῆς ἐξουσίας τοῦ Σατανᾶ ἐπὶ τὸν Θεόν, τοῦ λαβεῖν αὐτοὺς
ἄφεσιν ἁμαρτιῶν καὶ κλῆρον ἐν τοῖς ἡγιασμένοις πίστει τῇ εἰς ἐμέ.

Common to both passages are ἡ ἐξουσία τοῦ σκότους or
τοῦ Σατανᾶ, the idea of transference from this ἐξουσία to
God or to Christ's kingdom, and the collocation of the conceptions of the promised land (κλῆρος) and of forgiveness
(ἄφεσις) and of God's people (ἡγιασμένοι or ἅγιοι). Cf.
also Acts xxvi. 23 quoted on *v.* 18 below. Is St Paul in this
epistle using ideas which had indeed been with him from the
time of his call? In any case, behind some, at least, of the
ideas in both passages is the O.T.; cf. Deut. xxxiii. 3f.

(iii) It is impossible to draw with precision the lines
between the various shades of meaning of ἐξουσία—
'authority', 'right' (abstract), or 'an authority' (a civic, or
a supernatural, holder of authority), or 'realm', 'sphere'

(which appears to be suitable here, though Masson denies this sense). But it is profitable to compare some relevant phrases: Luke xxii. 53 αὕτη ἐστὶν ὑμῶν ἡ ὥρα καὶ ἡ ἐξουσία τοῦ σκότους; Eph. ii. 2 κατὰ τὸν ἄρχοντα τῆς ἐξουσίας τοῦ ἀέρος; Luke iv. 6 σοὶ δώσω τὴν ἐξουσίαν ταύτην ἅπασαν καὶ τὴν δόξαν αὐτῶν, ὅτι ἐμοὶ παραδέδοται; the Washington MS.'s addition to Mark xvi. 14: πεπλήρωται ὁ ὅρος τῶν ἐτῶν τῆς ἐξουσίας τοῦ Σατανᾶ; and the use (as in ii. 15 below, q.v.) of ἐξουσίαι as = '(demonic) authorities', 'powers'. See Foerster in *T.W.N.T.* *s.v.*

(iv) The contrast σκότος—φῶς is, of course, common in the Bible (add to the instances in (ii) and (iii) above, not only O.T. instances but the Johannine use and I Pet. ii. 9 τοῦ ἐκ σκότους ὑμᾶς καλέσαντος εἰς τὸ θαυμαστὸν αὐτοῦ φῶς), and indeed it would be surprising to find any religion in which this obvious but telling metaphor was ignored;[1] but what is striking is that here St Paul uses it (as it is some-times used in the Johannine writings) of the *present* condition of Christians—not of the *future* termination of the present night by the dawn of the day of the Lord (cf. Phil. ii. 15 ἐν οἷς φαίνεσθε ὡς φωστῆρες ἐν κόσμῳ...). God *has already* 'transferred' them (μετέστησεν) from the realm of darkness to the kingdom of his Son. See on iii. 1–4 below.

(v) τὴν βασιλείαν τοῦ Υἱοῦ τῆς ἀγάπης αὐτοῦ constitutes one of the few N.T. references to the kingdom of *Christ*. Whether St Paul intends by it the 'interim' period between the resurrection and the final manifestation of the kingdom of *God* is debatable. Perhaps the passage most favourable to this idea is I Cor. xv. 24–8, where Christ must reign until the total subjection of all enemies is complete, where-upon he is to hand over the kingdom to *God*, and himself be subject to him. Also, the references to the kingdom of God

---

[1] See The Manual of Discipline, iii–iv, in the Dead Sea Scrolls (e.g. in Dupont-Sommer, p. 122). Also compare xi. 7, 8 (in Dupont-Sommer, p. 144) with 'the inheritance of the saints'.

are mainly future, whereas this (as has been seen) is an accomplished fact (so Davies, *Paul*, pp. 295, 296). The reference in iv. 11 to the kingdom of God is a quite general one.

The phrase ὁ Υἱὸς τῆς ἀγάπης αὐτοῦ is probably a Semitic way of saying 'God's dear Son', and is reminiscent, then, of the divine voice at the Baptism and Transfiguration.

(vi) Our 'rescue' (or 'emancipation') is here equated with the forgiveness of sins, which illustrates very clearly how entirely moral and spiritual the conception of the kingdom of God or of Christ was for the disciples of Christ. There is no trace of a nationalistic Messianism in the N.T. conception; nor yet of fancies about 'escape' into immortality without a corresponding change of character (the kind of escape which may have been promised by the false teachers at Colossae). It may be precisely to guard against such false teaching that ἄφεσις (which, in the Pauline or 'near Pauline' writings, is only found here and in Eph. i. 7) is here equated with ἀπολύτρωσις (see Lohmeyer and Lightfoot). If so, either Eph. is a *mere* copy here, or is itself more polemical than is sometimes allowed.

15–23. *At this point, references to prayer and thanksgiving merge into a description of Christ, which, in its turn, leads back again to a contemplation of his reconciling work and of its results among the Christians who are addressed.*

This section contains the 'Great Christology' (for some discussion of which, see Introduction, pp. 3–6)—perhaps the most striking of all the Pauline expressions of conviction as to the status of Christ. The following are some salient matters of interest and importance.

(i) It is worth the effort to recall that these stupendous words apply (if they are indeed St Paul's own) to one who, only some thirty years before (and possibly less), had been crucified. The identification of that historical person—the Nazarene who had been ignominiously executed—with the subject of this description is staggering, and fairly cries out for some explanation.

(ii) The terms of the description are to a large extent reminiscent of the 'Wisdom Literature'—the Jewish writings which contain descriptions of the Wisdom, the Spirit, or the Word of God. The notes below indicate certain details of this comparison; but the most significant passages may be named at once: Job xxviii, Ps. xxxiii, Prov. viii, Ecclus. xxiv, Wisdom vii. Davies, *Paul*, pp. 147 ff., makes the interesting point that the 'Torah', or Law, was closely connected with Wisdom in Jewish thought; and that St Paul, finding in Christ the New Torah, naturally associated him also with the creative Wisdom of the Wisdom Literature. Creation and morality—natural and revealed religion—are thus linked.

(iii) In none of the earlier extant Pauline writings is the startling statement made that Christ is, as it were, the goal or purpose towards which the created world is destined to move (*v.* 16: τὰ πάντα not only δι' αὐτοῦ ἔκτισται, but also εἰς αὐτόν). So, too, in iii. 11, πάντα καὶ ἐν πᾶσιν applies to Christ, whereas previously (I Cor. xv. 28) it had been a description of God.

Contrast, then, with the εἰς αὐτὸν ἔκτισται of *v.* 16, Rom. xi. 36 (εἰς αὐτόν referring to God), and I Cor. viii. 6 εἷς Θεὸς ὁ Πατήρ, ἐξ οὗ τὰ πάντα καὶ ἡμεῖς εἰς αὐτόν, καὶ εἷς Κύριος Ἰησοῦς Χριστός, δι' οὗ τὰ πάντα καὶ ἡμεῖς δι' αὐτοῦ, where God is origin and goal, while Christ is medium and agent. In Heb. ii. 10 God is the one, δι' ὅν ('for whose sake') and also δι' οὗ ('through whom') are all things.

Thus St Paul is exceptionally daring in Colossians, and does not strictly limit himself to the 'distribution of parts' in the noble doxology of J. M. Neale's translation of Abelard's *O quanta qualia*:

'Low before him with our praises we fall,
　Of whom, and in whom, and through whom are all;
　Of whom, the Father; and through whom, the Son;
　In whom, the Spirit, with these ever One.'

Yet (as Percy points out, *Probleme*, pp. 71–5) in both
1 Cor. viii and Col. i alike, as also in Phil. ii, the main
emphasis is on the glory of God and the supremacy of Christ
over creation. When considering apparently divergent
passages, it is important to look at the purpose of the
wording before pronouncing on the details of the language.

(iv) The word πλήρωμα (*v.* 19) is notable: more is said on
this below and in the discursive note (p. 164).

(v) The description of Christ in his relation to the whole
created world and in his work in creation springs from, and
soon returns again to, the more particular matter of his
relation to the Church and his work of salvation. Christ is
both πρωτότοκος πάσης κτίσεως (*v.* 15) and πρωτότοκος ἐκ
τῶν νεκρῶν (*v.* 18). It is possible (so Dibelius) that the false
teachers accepted Christ, in a limited way, as one who could
rescue from sin, but doubted whether he had, as it were, the
freedom of the universe; they thought (possibly) that one
needed to make terms with other powers besides Christ, if
one's salvation from fate and from mortality was to be
complete. If so (but it cannot be proved), added point is
given to the inseparable unity here maintained between the
'cosmic' and the personal, the creative and the redemptive,
work of Christ. See on *v.* 18 below. This connexion between
creation and redemption is of undiminished importance still
—at a time when, in many quarters, there is a tendency to
drive a wedge between 'Nature' and 'Grace', and to
present Christ as an antithesis to Nature rather than as
Nature's completion and meaning. See Davies, *Paul*,
pp. 175f.

(vi) Masson has argued (much as H. J. Holtzmann in
1872, C. R. Bowen in *J.B.L.* vol. XLIII (1924), pp. 177ff.,
F. C. Porter, *The Mind of Christ in Paul* (Scribner's, 1932),
pp. 197f., and many others) that *vv.* 15–20 are a non-
Pauline composition. He takes them to be an early
Christian hymn of praise to Christ, slightly augmented by

the clause καὶ αὐτός ἐστιν ἡ κεφαλὴ τοῦ σώματος, τῆς ἐκκλησίας inserted here by the author of Ephesians. See Masson in his Commentary and in *Revue de Théologie et de Philosophie*, CXLVIII (1948), p. 140. Already Lohmeyer had put forward a comparable theory about Phil. ii, as containing a pre-Pauline hymn (*Kyrios Jesus*, in *Sitzungs-berichte d. Heidelberger Akad. d. Wiss., Phil.-hist. Klasse*, IV (1927–8)); and I Pet. iii. 18–22 has been correspondingly treated by Bultmann (see *The Theology of the New Testament*, translated by K. Grobel, S.C.M. 1955, ii, p. 153).

It is difficult to weigh such suggestions decisively. But it may be remarked that:

(*a*) Dibelius' reading of the situation (see (v) above) seems to give a plausible reason for the introduction at this point, by St Paul himself, though possibly in words drawn in part from some Hellenistic hymn to the Wisdom or Word of God, of some vindication of Christ's supremacy.

(*b*) Many of the arguments are very subjective—even Bowen's (who claims more objectivity than some), when he holds that (1) the kind of error here attacked is incom-patible with phrases elsewhere in the epistle which imply that the Church had been only recently founded; (2) the genuine Paul leaves us (as in Galatians) in no doubt about the nature of what he attacks; (3) the Christology is un-paralleled in the known Pauline writings; (4) the grammar is lax (a decidedly double-edged argument).

(*c*) Arguments based on rhythm, parallelism, and sup-posed strophic arrangement are precarious enough at the best of times, and most of all when there is no recognizable quantitative metre by which to judge.

Is it, then, so clear that this was a separate hymn—not to mention the question whether the 'head of the Church' clause is a further addition?

(*d*) The rarity elsewhere in the Paulines of certain words in a passage like this is not necessarily an indication of

spuriousness: one must ask, rather, whether there were any
better or more natural terms at the writer's disposal, if he
needed to introduce this particular theme; or whether there
are any words here which it seems impossible that St Paul
himself would have used. The idea of the reconciliation of
'all things' is perhaps the hardest to accommodate to the
rest of St Paul's thought: see notes on i. 20 and ii. 4–iii. 4.

(e) C. F. Burney ingeniously suggested that the passage
might be a meditation on Prov. viii. 22 with Gen. i. 1 in
the Rabbinic manner. If so, the need to call in extraneous,
Hellenistic sources to explain it is further reduced. (See
Burney, 'Christ as the APXH of Creation', *J.T.S.* xxvii
(1925–6), pp. 160 ff.; and summaries in A. E. J. Rawlinson,
The New Testament Doctrine of the Christ (Longmans, 1929),
p. 163, n. 5, and Davies, *Paul*, pp. 151 f.)

(f) It must be admitted that the relative pronoun ὅς in
vv. 15, 18 is not obviously natural, and might be taken to
indicate that a snatch of an already existing hymn or credal
formula was being quoted (cf. I Tim. iii. 16 ὅς ἐφανερώθη...).
Yet nobody can deny that it makes a perfectly correct and
logical sequence.

Thus, on the whole, the difficulties do not seem to warrant
the conjecture of interpolation.

Turning to details, the following are selected from a mass
of notable matters.

15. εἰκὼν τοῦ Θεοῦ τοῦ ἀοράτου. Christ is claimed to
gather up in his own person that manifestation of the
invisible God which was to be found both generally in
Nature (Rom. i. 20) and, more particularly, in Man. If
Man is 'in the image of God' (Gen. i. 26, I Cor. xi. 7,
II Cor. iii. 18, Col. iii. 10, cf. James iii. 9), then so is Christ
par. excellence. He is the perfect likeness of God, whereas
carved images, abhorred by the Jews, are blasphemous
counterfeits.

Already in II Cor. iv. 4 St Paul had used this term (ὅς

ἐστιν εἰκὼν τοῦ Θεοῦ); and it is familiar enough to students of ancient thought, from Philo. Thus, in *de Vit. Mos.* II. 65, cited by Dibelius, man is εἰκὼν τῆς ἀοράτου φύσεως ἐμφανής, ἀιδίου γενητή. But Philo uses εἰκών also of the heavenly Wisdom, *Leg. All.* I. 43, and of the Logos, *de Conf.* 97 and 147, etc.; and it is applied to the Spirit or Wisdom of God in Wisdom vii. 26, which was perhaps written about A.D. 40 and may have been known to St Paul (see W. L. Knox, *Jerusalem*, pp. 128f. for parallels, though it is a question whether they reflect more than a common fund of ideas). The language of Heb. i. 3 bears the same stamp. It is obvious enough language to use in allusion to the visible signs of God's wise ordering of his world and of creation. See further W. L. Knox, *Gentiles*, p. 159 nn.

But what follows in the present context shows that to Christ it is applied in a unique way.

πρωτότοκος πάσης κτίσεως. If this phrase were interpreted without reference to its context and to other expressions of St Paul's thought about Christ, it might be natural to understand it as describing Christ as included among created things, and as merely the 'eldest' of that 'family': in Rom. viii. 29 πρωτότοκος does appear in this included sense—εἰς τὸ εἶναι αὐτὸν πρωτότοκον ἐν πολλοῖς ἀδελφοῖς. And so it was interpreted by the Arian disputants in the Arian controversy (see Lightfoot *in loc.*). A comparable ambiguity of phrase is found in Rev. iii. 14, where ἡ ἀρχὴ τῆς κτίσεως could (merely in itself and without taking wider considerations into account) mean 'the first among created things'. The similar word πρωτόγονος is used in this included sense in a fragment of the Jewish *Prayer of Joseph* in Origen, *Comm. in Joh.* ii. 31 (see Windisch, *Weisheit*, p. 225 n.); and in the 'Hermetic' writings it appears in a similar sense (see Dodd, *F.G.*, p. 15, n. 1).

Yet to interpret πρωτότοκος in this included sense here would simply be inconsistent—not only with the immediately following words about Christ's agency in creation (implying his priority to it) and with similar references elsewhere (see above), but also with the conception of Christ as the divine and pre-existent Wisdom, and with the Christian experience of redemption, which cannot be accounted for in terms of a Redeemer who is included among created things: it demands the postulate of divine action. (In Rom. viii. 29, just quoted, the point is a different one.)

Accordingly, interpretation seems to be confined to the following alternatives:

(i) Translate the πρωτό- as a *time-metaphor*. See John i. 30 πρῶτός μου ἦν, and II Kingd. (=II Sam.) xix. 44 πρωτότοκος ἐγὼ ἢ σύ (though that may mean, not 'I was born before you' but 'I am the first-born rather than you': see A. W. Argyle and H. G. Meecham in *E.T.* LXVI, no. 2 (Nov. 1954), no. 4 (Jan. 1955), and no. 10 (July 1955)). Translated thus, it may allude to Christ's priority to the created world: he was born (or, as more considered theology would say, begotten, not born) before any created thing, like the Wisdom, to which Burney saw a reference (above, (vi) (*e*)).

(ii) Take 'firstborn' not as a temporal term so much as in the sense of *supreme*—'the one who is supreme over all creation'. In *v.* 18 below, πρωτεύων seems to mean something similar, although in that verse ἀρχή and πρωτότοκος evidently refer to a different conception, namely the conception of Christ as the pioneer for others who were to follow, exactly as in Rom. viii. 29, Heb. i. 6, Rev. i. 5; and cf. Heb. xii. 23, where the πρωτότοκοι are, perhaps, Christians as destined to lead the way, in Christ, for others (unless, with Lightfoot on Colossians, we take the allusion there to be to Christians as 'heirs of the kingdom').

If one must choose, there is, perhaps, a little more to be said in favour of (ii), in view of the πρωτεύων of *v.* 18 and of such O.T. antecedents as Ps. lxxxix. 27 (LXX lxxxviii. 28) κἀγὼ πρωτότοκον θήσομαι αὐτόν. But possibly (i) and (ii) are to be combined: 'prior to and supreme over'. See discussions in Davies, *Paul*, pp. 150 ff. and V. Taylor, *Names*, pp. 147 ff. In Rabbinic thought, God is described as the one who preceded time (S.-B. *in loc.*); and commentators quote Rabbi Bechai as calling God himself the 'Firstborn of the World'! But R. Bechai appears to be R. Baḥya ben Asher, a late writer (died 1340), who is scarcely important for the original meaning of our passage.

16. ἐν αὐτῷ is possibly both instrumental and local—'by means of him and within him'. As Lightfoot says, 'the Judaeo-Alexandrine teachers represented the Logos...as the τόπος where the eternal ideas, the νοητὸς κόσμος, had their abode' (he adduces Philo, *de Opif.* 17 and 20).

εἴτε θρόνοι κ.τ.λ. θρόνοι and κυριότητες are evidently supernatural potentates of some sort, and so, probably, are ἀρχαί and ἐξουσίαι. For the latter pair, see further on ii. 15 below. Meanwhile, note the following allusions to these potentates (adduced by various commentators): Ethiopic Enoch (I Enoch) xli. 9 ('angel', 'power'), lxi. 10 ('all the angels of power', 'all the angels of principalities'); Slavonic Enoch (II Enoch) xx. 1 ('dominions', 'governments', 'thrones', etc., in the seventh heaven); Testaments of the XII Patriarchs, Levi iii. 8 (θρόνοι, ἐξουσίαι); Ascension of Isaiah (trans. R. H. Charles, A. and C. Black, 1900) vii. 21 (ἄγγελοι, ἀρχάγγελοι, κυριότητες, θρόνοι); Acts of John 79, 98, 104, 114. Also (Lightfoot) Origen *de Princ.* i. 5. 3, i. 6. 2, Ephrem Syrus *Opera* (Rome, 1737) i. p. 270 (on Deut. i. 13) and Basil of Seleucia *Orat.* xxxix. 207.

Theodoret *in loc.*, and several of the Fathers, interpret the 'thrones' as the 'cherubim' (or winged, gryphon-like creatures which supported God's throne in Ezek. i), and the κυριότητες, ἀρχαί, and ἐξουσίαι as the guardian angels of the nations (cf. Dan. x. 13, 20). But more probably (according to Lightfoot) the reference is to the occupants of the thrones which, in apocalyptic imagery, surround the throne of God (see Origen just cited).

In any case, the cumulative effect of this catalogue of powers is to emphasize the immeasurable superiority of Christ over whatever rivals might, by the false teachers, be suggested: he is himself the agent and the place of their creation, and their very *raison d'être*. In the parallel passage, Eph. i. 21, Christ is raised by God ὑπεράνω πάσης ἀρχῆς καὶ ἐξουσίας καὶ δυνάμεως καὶ κυριότητος καὶ παντὸς ὀνόματος ὀνομαζομένου οὐ μόνον ἐν τῷ αἰῶνι τούτῳ ἀλλὰ καὶ ἐν τῷ μέλλοντι. Cf. I Pet. iii. 22 ὑποταγέντων αὐτῷ ἀγγέλων καὶ ἐξουσιῶν καὶ δυνάμεων.

17. αὐτός ἐστιν πρὸ πάντων. Two questions arise:

(i) Is αὐτός ἐστιν to be thus accented—making ἐστιν a mere copula connecting αὐτός with πρὸ πάντων—or to be accented αὐτὸς ἔστιν—making ἔστιν = 'he exists'? (The virtual absence of accentuation in the most ancient MSS. leaves one free to choose.) In favour of the latter is the fact that John viii. 58 (πρὶν Ἀβραὰμ γενέσθαι ἐγὼ εἰμί) seems to show that the N.T. includes within its scope the conception of Christ's 'absolute' existence; but whether St Paul is likely to have intended so metaphysical a phrase and to have used the paradoxical present tense (instead of a more temporal ἦν) is less certain.

(ii) Does πρό refer to priority in time or in rank? However we interpret the verb, are we to continue '*before* all things' or '*superior to* all things'? It is the same problem as with πρωτότοκος in v. 15 above. Judging by linguistic analogies, temporal priority is here the more likely sense, for (*a*) πρό seems never to be used of priority in *importance* except in πρὸ πάντων ('above all') as in Jas. v. 12, I Pet. iv. 8, and in epistolary formulae adduced by M.M. *s.v.* (cf. περὶ πάντων in III John 2); and (*b*) more likely ways of expressing priority in importance would be (as Lightfoot points out) ἐπὶ πάντων, or ὑπὲρ πάντα or ὑπεράνω πάντων. In favour of priority of importance is the fact that both the πρωτότοκος of *v*. 15 and the πρωτεύων of *v*. 18 may bear this meaning; but even if they do, that does not bind the present phrase to that sense.

The choice, then, must be from: 'he exists before...', 'he exists as supreme over...', 'he is before...', 'he is supreme over...'; and if the evidence favours 'before', then 'exists' is the more logical.

τὰ πάντα ἐν αὐτῷ συνέστηκεν. 'The universe owes its coherence to him.' In the same vein, the Spirit of God is described in Wisdom i. 7 as τὸ συνέχον τὰ πάντα, 'that which holds everything together'. So in Ecclus. xliii. 26 ἐν λόγῳ αὐτοῦ σύγκειται τὰ πάντα. Cf. Heb. i. 3, where Christ is the 'strength and stay upholding all creation', φέρων τε τὰ πάντα....

18. ἡ κεφαλὴ τοῦ σώματος, τῆς ἐκκλησίας. The description of Christ as the Head of the Body, that is, of the Church, is exactly paralleled in Eph. i. 22, 23 (see also Col. ii. 19, Eph. iv. 15), but not in the earlier Pauline epistles, where instead the implications are that he is not the head but the body itself (I Cor. x. 16, 17, xii. 12, 27, cf. Rom. xii. 5) as constituted by his 'members'.

Some commentators regard this difference as important. H. Schlier (*T.W.N.T. s. κεφαλή*), for instance, discerned in Ephesians a clear echo of the type of thought represented by the later Gnostic systems in which the earthly 'body' of mankind has a heavenly 'head' in the person of its Saviour; and K. L. Schmidt (in *T.W.N.T. s. ἐκκλησία*) asserts that the Body-and-Head conception is not a natural development from I Corinthians and Romans. It does not, however, appear to be a sufficiently abstruse idea to drive one to look for its origin elsewhere than in the early Church's experience. I have found no allusion to this 'Head' conception in Rabbinical sources (as cited in S.-B. or Davies,

Paul), but 'the Head' is a common enough O.T. expression for 'the chief' or 'the leader', or 'the origin'; and in a context where the supremacy of Christ is prominent, precisely because it had been challenged by the Colossian error, what is more natural than to refer to the Church as subject to Christ, as is also the whole universe? 'The name "the Head" asserts His inseparability from the Church, but excludes His identity with it' (V. Taylor, *Names*, pp. 101 f.).

If, however, we explain this usage here by reference to the situation in the Lycus valley communities, we must, of course, think again when we come to Ephesians. But that is not our immediate task. In any case, it must not be assumed that, to St Paul, κεφαλή suggested *control* or *direction* as by the mind. It is true (see Lightfoot) that this function of the brain had already been suggested by Hippocrates and at least tentatively accepted by Plato; but it appears to have been obscured by Aristotle and then by the Stoics; and it is safer to assume that, to St Paul, it meant *supremacy* and, perhaps, *origin*. See S. Bedale in *J.T.S.* n.s. v, no. 2 (Oct. 1954), pp. 211 ff.

More striking, in fact, is the earlier equation of Christ with the whole Body. The evidence suggests that the metaphorical use of 'body' as meaning a society or a collection of parts had never been common (even if Stoic, Gnostic, and Rabbinic instances are found): 'it did not of itself suggest a social group' (Robinson, *The Body*, p. 50). But St Paul takes the word σῶμα and uses it not merely to mean 'a collection of people' (as though it were τὸ σῶμα τῶν Χριστιανῶν) but to designate Christians as 'the organism which belongs to Christ' (τὸ σῶμα τοῦ Χριστοῦ)—his very own Body (see Davies, *Paul*, p. 57, and T. W. Manson quoted above, *Introd.*, p. 6). This is overwhelmingly impressive, and theologically of the greatest possible importance. See Introduction, pp. 6 f.

It is noteworthy that here and in *v.* 24 ἐκκλησία evidently means not a local congregation only, but the entire Church. See A Note on Christian Greetings in Letters, p. 154.

ἀρχή. See on *v.* 15 above. The word has a perplexing number of associations: it is highly suggestive. Does it refer to Christ's *supremacy in rank* (cf. πρωτότοκος *v.* 15 and note), or to his *precedence in time* (cf. on *vv.* 15 and 17 above), or to his *creative initiative* (cf. Burney, under vi (*e*) in the introductory notes to *vv.* 15–23)? Moreover, if the last suggestion is adopted, two further alternatives come into view—is this creative initiative related to the creation of the *universe* or to the 'new creation', the creation of the redeemed community, the *Christian Church*? (cf. Bedale, just cited).

On balance, the context seems to support the latter. That in Rev. iii. 14 ἀρχή is used in the 'cosmic' sense is no argument against it; and πρωτότοκος ἐκ τῶν νεκρῶν (cf. Rev. i. 5 ὁ π. τῶν νεκρῶν) undoubtedly points to this sense, and cf. Acts xxvi. 23 εἰ πρῶτος ἐξ ἀναστάσεως νεκρῶν φῶς μέλλει καταγγέλλειν κ.τ.λ. If this interpretation is right, then the theme of this verse lends some plausibility to the attempt of the ancient commentators to interpret πρωτότοκος πάσης κτίσεως in *v.* 15 similarly—of God's *new* creation the Church, rather than of the 'cosmos'. But it is generally agreed that they were mistaken there; and it is better to reckon with the two themes—creation in *v.* 15, re-creation (that is, salvation) in *v.* 18—and so to find a striking instance of how 'cosmology' and 'soteriology' are interlaced. Cf. remark (v) in the introduction to this section and note on Col. iii. 14 below. Both parts of this 'Great Christology' carry in them the phrase ὅς ἐστιν...πρωτότοκος (*vv.* 15, 18).

ἵνα γένηται ἐν πᾶσιν αὐτὸς πρωτεύων. It may be that αὐτός here means 'himself alone' (for instances of this sense, see L. and S., *s.v.*). Whether ἐν πᾶσιν means 'in all respects' or 'among all things' is not clear. But the latter is, perhaps, the more likely in the context, so that the whole phrase will mean: 'that he might be alone supreme among all'—sole head of the whole of things. (I owe this interpretation to a remark of Dr J. A. T. Robinson's.)

19. ὅτι ἐν αὐτῷ εὐδόκησεν πᾶν τὸ πλήρωμα κατοικῆσαι. The two chief questions arising over this famous phrase are:

(i) What does πᾶν τὸ πλήρωμα mean?

(ii) What is the subject of εὐδόκησεν? Is it πᾶν τὸ πλήρωμα, or Christ, or God?

(i) Reasons are given in A Note on πλήρωμα, p. 164, for believing that Christ is thought of as containing, representing, all that God is; and for interpreting πᾶν τὸ πλήρωμα here as 'God in all his fulness'.

(ii) What is the subject of εὐδόκησεν?

The answer seems to be either πᾶν τὸ πλήρωμα or God— not Christ; for although it is true that the broad analogies seem to be equally balanced, and, as far as such evidence goes, we are therefore free to choose either (in II Cor. v. 18f. the Father is the one who reconciles, in Eph. ii. 16 it is the Son), yet the ἐν αὐτῷ (i.e. in Christ) makes it initially unlikely that Christ himself is the subject (see A Note on the Reflexive Pronoun, p. 169).

As between πᾶν τὸ πλήρωμα and God, the choice is more difficult. On balance, πᾶν τὸ πλήρωμα seems slightly the better claimant, for:

(a) It is difficult to take God as the subject, since v. 13 is the last verse in which he is clearly the subject of a verb; some renewed mention might, therefore, be expected if this were intended.

(b) If πᾶν τὸ πλήρωμα may be taken as a periphrasis for 'God in all his fulness', the subsequent masculines, εἰς αὐτόν (as = 'to himself', see A Note on the Reflexive Pronoun, p. 169) and εἰρηνοποιήσας, may be explained as a construction according to sense—masculine because, on this showing, πλήρωμα stands for a masculine. Moreover, in ii. 9 πᾶν τὸ

πλ. τῆς Θεότητος is certainly the subject of κατοικεῖ. The
only question is whether, in the present context and with
πλήρωμα used absolutely, the personification is not too
violent to be credible.

In either case, there does not appear to be much difficulty
in returning to Christ as subject at *v.* 22 (as is necessary);
and although, admittedly, the return in *v.* 20 to τοῦ σταυροῦ
αὐτοῦ is harsh, yet to take Christ as subject (avoiding this
latter harshness and a change of subject in *vv.* 19f.) multi-
plies reflexives to an improbable extent.

20. ἀποκαταλλάξαι τὰ πάντα.... 'To reconcile' is
properly a verb which (except in the language of actuaries
or of logic) relates exclusively to persons; and the idea of
reconciling to God 'everything'—the animate and the
inanimate alike—is a difficult one for the modern reader
(although *v.* 16 above seems to suggest that St Paul readily
resolved τὰ πάντα into personal beings). Still more striking
is the application, to the same all-inclusive field, of the
idea of peace-making through the blood of the cross—that
is, through Christ's death viewed in terms of sacrifice (and
possibly with associations recalling also the covenant of
God with man). The peace which is made and the enmity
which is slain upon the cross in Eph. ii. 15, 16 are between
Jew and Gentile—which is a more intelligible idea, and
which is taken up also in the present passage in *vv.* 21 ff. But
Colossians includes the 'cosmic' scene as well as the scene
of man's salvation throughout this passage. Perhaps the
best comment on this inclusive hope is Rom. viii, with its
promise of redemption for (apparently) Nature as well as
Man. Compare (with Best, *One Body*, p. 116) the harmony
of Nature in Isa. xi. 6–9. See further on ii. 4–iii. 4 below.

21. καὶ ὑμᾶς κ.τ.λ. Clearly an address to Gentiles—who
had been estranged from God's family and at enmity both
inwardly, in their 'attitude' or 'outlook' or cast of mind,
and outwardly, in their wicked practices. For τῇ διανοίᾳ

cf. Eph. iv. 18 and Luke i. 51. In the latter, does διανοίᾳ καρδίας go with ὑπερηφάνους ('haughty-minded') or with διεσκόρπισεν ('he scattered them in the midst of their intentions')?

ἐχθρούς probably means 'hostile', not 'hated': 'It is the mind of man, not the mind of God, which must undergo a change'—Lightfoot.

22. νυνὶ δὲ.... Text and punctuation are both uncertain. The simplest is to put a stop at the end of v. 20 and read ἀποκατήλλαξεν. The παραστῆσαι in v. 22 may then be treated as a consecutive (or even final) infinitive: 'you who were estranged...he has nevertheless (δέ) now reconciled ...so as to present you....' The δέ, though strictly un-grammatical, is then intelligible, as though it had been preceded by καὶ ὑμεῖς ποτε μὲν ἦτε....

But ἀποκατήλλαξεν (so most MSS.) may be only an intelligent correction of a passive indicative or participle (ἀποκατηλλάγητε (p⁴⁶) B (33) Ephr; ἀποκαταλλαγέντες D* G m Ir—bracketed witnesses represent slight variants in spelling). To accept the passive indicative would involve either adopting W.H.'s parenthesis punctuation (they make a parenthesis of νυνὶ...τοῦ θανάτου), which will also make sense with the active; or removing the stop from the end of v. 20, and putting one after πονηροῖς (v. 21). But this latter involves taking καὶ ὑμᾶς κ.τ.λ. as a clumsy afterthought to the sentence of v. 20, and treating the ὑμᾶς of v. 22 as reflexive ('yourselves'). The passive participle is harder still. The original reading may have contained a passive, but if so it has been well mended.

ἐν τῷ σώματι τῆς σαρκὸς αὐτοῦ. The phrase may simply be used to indicate that the historical body of Jesus is meant, not his 'mystical' body, the Church. But it is vital to the Gospel that Christ suffered physically, and not in appearance merely, as the 'docetic' type of teaching maintained: and this, too, may be intended by the phrase. See on ii. 11 f. below.

παραστῆσαι ὑμᾶς.... Unless (with the W.H. punctuation alluded to above) this infinitive is construed (like ἀποκαταλλάξαι in *v.* 20) with εὐδόκησεν, it is an open question whether it represents a final or a consecutive idea— 'in order to present' or 'so as to present'. In any case, the presenting is in fact a consequence of Christ's death. It is here perhaps a sacrificial metaphor (though in *v.* 28 below this is not so likely), as is suitable to ἁγίους καὶ ἀμώμους: united with Christ in his self-sacrifice, those who are reconciled are thought of as themselves a sacrifice to God; cf. Rom. xii. 1 and Phil. ii. 17. It is possible also (see Lightfoot) that κατενώπιον αὐτοῦ refers to the bringing of the sacrifice into God's presence for approval rather than to the Last Judgment. This voluntary self-identification of Christians with Christ's offering of his obedience is essential to the N.T. conception of reconciliation: Christ does for us what we could not do for ourselves; but we must do, for our part, what he will not do for us. He 'offers' us to God, but it is none the less our own offering.

23. The section ends with a reference to ideal Christian firmness (cf. the parable of the two houses, Matt. vii. 24–7), and to the scope of the Gospel, as in ii. 5 and i. 6 respectively. To proclaim the Gospel 'in the whole of creation' evidently meant, for St Paul, not necessarily to reach every individual with the Good News, but to let it be heard in all the great centres of the Empire (cf. Rom. xv. 19–23). That this had already been done probably confirmed the apostle in his expectation that the consummation of God's plan was not far off. Compare with this the injunction to world-wide teaching in Matt. xxviii. 19, and the statement that this must take place before 'the end' (Mark xiii. 10, etc.). See J. Munck, 'Israel and the Gentiles in the New Testament', *J.T.S.* (n.s.) I, no. 1 (April 1951). κτίσις in the present passage seems to mean 'the whole world', 'everybody' (parallel to πᾶς ὁ κόσμος in i. 6), exactly as in Mark xvi. 15

πορευθέντες εἰς τὸν κόσμον ἅπαντα κηρύξατε τὸ εὐαγγέλιον πάσῃ τῇ κτίσει. But in i. 15 κτίσις appears to mean, more generally, 'the created universe' (cf. Mark x. 6 etc. ἀπὸ δὲ ἀρχῆς κτίσεως...).

διάκονος. Cf. iv. 7, 17 below. In the N.T. this is still a very general term, by no means limited to the technical sense of 'deacon'; it is applied to those who are engaged in service of any sort (in Rom. xv. 8—and cf. διακονῆσαι in Mark x. 45—it is applied to Christ himself).

i. 24–ii. 3. *The apostle's share in the reconciling work of God in Christ.*

From the contemplation of Christ's relation to the work of God both in the creation of the world and in the 'new creation' which is the redeemed community, the Christian Church, St Paul passes on to the subject of his own share in it. I am proud and glad, he says, to undergo physical suffering in the work of evangelism. It is my contribution to the quota of sufferings which the whole Church must undergo in the working out of God's designs. For that work of evangelism I have been commissioned by God. It means proclaiming to you without reserve that secret which has been kept hidden from all previous generations but is now divulged to God's people—the precious and glorious secret which consists of Christ, and of the fact that Christ, the Jews' Messiah, is among you who are Gentiles, and has given you a firm basis for confident expectation of a glorious destiny. It is the task of us who are evangelists to proclaim him, with admonition and teaching and insight, so as to bring each one of our friends as a mature Christian into the presence of God. That is the object of my struggles and toil, which I achieve by virtue of God's strength within me; and, although we have never met one another personally, I want you to know how I struggle for you with a view to your being brought to a mature and stable Christian character, built upon Christ, God's ' secret', in whom are included all the stores of God's wisdom.

24. Νῦν. Some texts (including D* E* FG—not p⁴⁶) prefix a relative pronoun, ὅς. The νῦν is certainly abrupt without it, but that may be the very reason for its insertion by a scribe, coupled, perhaps, with the temptation to the eye to repeat the last syllable of διάκονος (see Lightfoot); and with it the sentence is very long.

It is not obvious, in any case, what the force of νῦν is. Lightfoot interprets it to mean 'now, when I see all the glory of bearing a part in this magnificent work'—in contrast to any temptation which St Paul may previously have felt to repine at his lot. Others (e.g. Peake and Masson) refer it to his present condition as a prisoner: formerly he could rejoice in 'active service', now he will rejoice in the sufferings of imprisonment, recognizing them as a contribution to evangelism. The latter seems to receive little support from the context, which is largely concerned with active preaching and teaching (as though imprisonment were regarded as only an incident in the evangelist's varied life of toils and hazards); and to this extent Lightfoot's suggestion is preferable. Easier still (if it were permissible) would be to assume that νῦν is merely a connecting or resumptive particle (rather like τοίνυν)—'and so'; but there seems to be no evidence for such a use.

χαίρω ἐν τοῖς παθήμασιν.... For a general parallel, see Eph. iii. 13. But the present passage offers peculiar difficulties. What is meant by 'filling up what is lacking of the afflictions of (the) Christ'?

One thing is clear—that St Paul, like the other N.T. writers, regarded the actual death of Jesus as efficacious and complete and once-for-all (see Col. ii. 11, 12, to go no further afield). It cannot, then, be in this regard that he finds any ὑστερήματα. 'St Paul would have been the last to say that [Christians] bear their part in the atoning sacrifice of Christ' (Lightfoot).

It does not seem plausible, either, to interpret the sentence to mean that what is lacking is the *availability* of the *benefits* of Christ's afflictions, as though the apostle's sufferings were regarded as the necessary friction in the wire which is transmitting the power from the dynamo. This may indeed be a genuine aspect of Christian suffering, which does help to make available what God in Christ has done; but the words here hardly admit of such an interpretation.

Two main types of interpretation, then, fall to be considered:

(i) Christ's sufferings (on the cross and throughout his ministry) are necessarily shared by Christians, οἱ ἐν Χριστῷ: their union with him involves their participation in his sufferings. 'What is lacking' might then = 'what is yet to be shared, what is still due to us'—no Christian still in this life having yet completed the tale of suffering which his union with the Suffering Servant implies. The continuance and ultimate completion of these sufferings, being a part of the privilege of incorporation in the Body of Christ, is something which the apostle welcomes.

(ii) There is a 'quota' of sufferings which 'the corporate Christ', the Messianic community, the Church, is destined to undergo before the purposes of God are complete. Accordingly, the more the apostle suffers in the cause of Christ and in the course of his ministry, the greater is his contribution to the coming of the End: he is thereby hastening 'the Day'.

On the whole, commentators range themselves on one side or the other. For my part, I am inclined to believe that the two should be combined, although I believe that, of the two, the second is the more uniformly probable and is the dominant idea, and that τὰ ὑστερήματα τῶν θλίψεων τοῦ Χριστοῦ is most likely to carry, as its primary meaning (overtones apart), 'what is yet to come of the afflictions of the (corporate) Christ', before the End. This is not incompatible with at least thus much of the first idea, that these 'Messianic woes' are themselves, in a sense, the sufferings of Jesus on the cross—of τοῦ Χριστοῦ in the sense of 'Jesus Christ', since the Messianic community, incorporated in Christ, are one with him: their sufferings are his, his are theirs.

The interpretation of ἀνταναπληρῶ must, obviously, be a factor in decision. But before we come to this, here are some data and references:

(a) θλῖψις is nowhere in the N.T. demonstrably used of the actual sufferings of Jesus on the cross or in his ministry.

(b) The following quotations are relevant to the general theme of the Christians' share in the sufferings of Christ:

II Cor. i. 5 καθὼς περισσεύει τὰ παθήματα τοῦ Χριστοῦ εἰς ἡμᾶς...; 6f. ἐν ὑπομονῇ τῶν αὐτῶν παθημάτων ὧν καὶ ἡμεῖς πάσχομεν...κοινωνοί ἐστε τῶν παθημάτων...; iv. 12 ὁ θάνατος ἐν ἡμῖν ἐνεργεῖται (i.e. the apostle is undergoing spiritually a 'death' like Christ's); xi. 29 (an example of the apostle taking distress upon himself) τίς ἀσθενεῖ, καὶ οὐκ ἀσθενῶ; τίς σκανδαλίζεται, καὶ οὐκ ἐγὼ πυροῦμαι; xiii. 4 καὶ γὰρ ἡμεῖς ἀσθενοῦμεν ἐν αὐτῷ...; Phil. i. 29f. ὅτι ὑμῖν ἐχαρίσθη τὸ ὑπὲρ Χριστοῦ, οὐ μόνον τὸ εἰς αὐτὸν πιστεύειν ἀλλὰ καὶ τὸ ὑπὲρ αὐτοῦ πάσχειν...; iii. 10 γνῶναι...κοινωνίαν παθημάτων αὐτοῦ; I Pet. iv. 13 καθὸ κοινωνεῖτε τοῖς τοῦ Χριστοῦ παθήμασιν χαίρετε,...; v. 9 εἰδότες τὰ αὐτὰ τῶν παθημάτων τῇ ἐν τῷ κόσμῳ ὑμῶν ἀδελφότητι ἐπιτελεῖσθαι...; Rev. i. 9 ἐγὼ Ἰωάνης, ὁ ἀδελφὸς ὑμῶν καὶ συνκοινωνὸς ἐν τῇ θλίψει καὶ βασιλείᾳ καὶ ὑπομονῇ ἐν Ἰησοῦ.

(c) The following considerations are relevant to the idea of a 'quota' of sufferings before the End:

Matt. xxiv. 6 etc., Mark xiii. 8 etc., Luke xxi. 9 etc. all speak of sufferings which are to precede the End (and so do Jewish apocalypses); and Luke xxi. 24, in particular, suggests a fixed period of time, ἄχρι οὗ πληρωθῶσιν καιροὶ ἐθνῶν. So II Thess. ii reckons with a period of tribulation. Similarly Heb. xi. 40, ἵνα μὴ χωρὶς ἡμῶν τελειωθῶσιν, suggests that the sufferings of the former heroes of faith required to be supplemented by those of the Christian Church before the process was complete; and in Rev. vi. 11 the

Christian martyrs are told that there are other martyrdoms yet to come before the quota is complete: ἕως πληρωθῶσιν καὶ οἱ σύνδουλοι αὐτῶν.... Again, in Rom. xi. 25, the phrase ἄχρι οὗ τὸ πλήρωμα τῶν ἐθνῶν εἰσέλθῃ bears witness to the idea of a predetermined quota of persons to be converted— which links up with the idea (present in our Colossians passage) that *evangelism* is the key to the process. In a sense, besides a quota of sufferings and a quota of persons, there is also (ironically speaking, perhaps) a quota of wickedness to be completed: Matt. xxiii. 32, I Thess. ii. 16.

To isolate such phrases would be to lay an unbalanced stress on predestinarian ideas. But they do show that St Paul and his contemporaries were familiar with this way of looking at things: a definite quantity, known to God, if hidden from men, of sins, sufferings, and conversions must precede the End. 'Fixa est mensura passionum, quas tota exantlare debet ecclesia. Quo plus igitur exhausit, eo minus et ipsi posthac et caeteris relinquitur' is Bengel's comment (*Gnomon N.T., in loc.*).

ἀνταναπληρῶ κ.τ.λ.

(i) Possibly Wettstein is right (*pace* Lightfoot) in his simple comment 'ἀντὶ ὑστερήματος succedit ἀνταναπλήρωμα', i.e. the ἀναπλήρωμα implied by the verb is to take the place (ἀντί) of the ὑστέρημα—instead of emptiness, fulness. Cf. II Cor. viii. 14 τὸ ὑμῶν περίσσευμα εἰς τὸ ἐκείνων ὑστέρημα; ix. 12 προσαναπληροῦσα τὰ ὑστερήματα...; xi. 9 τὸ γὰρ ὑστέρημά μου προσανεπλήρωσαν...(in both the latter, προσ- is comparable to ἀντι- here). There is no LXX occurrence of ἀνταναπληροῦν. In Wisdom xix. 4 προσαναπληροῦν occurs, in some MSS., of the Egyptians, who, by their folly, completed what was still lacking in their punishment for oppressing the Israelites:...ἵνα τὴν λείπουσαν ταῖς βασάνοις προσαναπληρώσωσιν κόλασιν....

(ii) More probably, however, the ἀντι- is only a redundant repetition of the ὑπέρ which precedes it. It is then

part of the idea that any sufferings which a Christian under-
goes as a Christian are a contribution *on behalf of* the whole
Body (cf. Acts ix. 16...ὅσα δεῖ αὐτὸν ὑπὲρ τοῦ ὀνόματός μου
παθεῖν; and Eph. iii. 1, 13). That ἀντί and ὑπέρ may be very
close in meaning is indicated by I Tim. ii. 6 ἀντίλυτρον ὑπὲρ
πάντων; and verbs are frequently, of course, compounded
with one preposition and preceded or followed by another.

On this showing ὑπὲρ ὑμῶν, though strictly referring to
the Colossians or the Lycus valley churches, must not be
confined to them: they are, in this context, representative of
others. If there is any particularization, it may be that
Gentiles are intended (as represented by the Colossians), for
St Paul's sufferings were incurred largely as a result of his
apostleship to them.

Of the extensive literature on various aspects of this
passage the following may be noted, besides the commentaries: Thornton, *Common Life*, pp. 34f., 304ff.; V.
Taylor, *The Atonement in New Testament Teaching* (Epworth
Press, 2nd ed., 1945); Robinson, *The Body*; George, *Communion*, p. 184; Best, *One Body*, pp. 134–6; R. Bultmann,
'Ignatius und Paulus' in *Studia Paulina*; Seidensticker, *Opfer*,
pp. 248f.

It may be added that, just as πλήρωμα was, in 'Gnostic'
contexts, a technical term (see A Note on πλήρωμα, p. 164), so
was ὑστέρημα. The Marcosians (a Gnostic sect of later days)
spoke of escaping διὰ τῆς γνώσεως τὴν τῶν ἐνενήκοντα ἐννέα
χώραν, τουτέστι τὸ ὑστέρημα (Iren. *adv. Haer.* i. 9. 2, Harvey's
ed.; = Migne xvi. 2, cited by Casey, as in A Note on the
Knowledge of God, p. 159); and the Valentinian system
spoke of κένωμα, 'the void', in antithesis to πλήρωμα (see
Lightfoot). In Epiph. *Haer.* 31. 16. 1, to be ἐν σκιᾶς καὶ
κενώματος τόποις means to be ἔξω...φωτὸς...καὶ πληρώματος (cited by Delling, in *T.W.N.T.* on πλήρης etc.).
If the false teachers at Colossae used ὑστέρημα in some
technical sense, Paul may be deliberately using their word;

but this is only guess-work. In Rom. xi. 12 the opposite to
πλήρωμα (in the sense 'completion') is παράπτωμα or
ἥττημα.

ἐν τῇ σαρκί μου ὑπὲρ τοῦ σώματος αὐτοῦ. Broadly
speaking (and with notable exceptions) the tendency, at
least with St Paul, is to use σάρξ for the realm in which
suffering and dying takes place. But to suffer in obedience
to God's will is to contribute to the building up of a durable
community which will transcend that realm of σάρξ. So
Christ's own sufferings in the realm of the σάρξ are redemptive for his corporate Body, the Church (cf., perhaps, ii. 11
below). But note that in the Words of Institution σῶμα,
not σάρξ, is used (see I Cor. xi. 24 and the Synoptic
parallels. But σάρξ is used in John vi).

25. κατὰ τὴν οἰκονομίαν κ.τ.λ., 'in virtue of the task
assigned by God to me for your benefit, namely the task of
fully proclaiming God's message'. οἰκονομία is either the
position of an administrator (such as a steward or foreman)
or the *activity* of thus administering—the exercise of this
office. But since the apostle knows that his apostolic office
(that of dispensing the Gospel) is in its turn dispensed to
him by God himself, it is very possible that οἰκονομία carries
in it also an allusion to *God's* administration. Cf. Eph. iii. 2
(a close parallel to the present passage), and Eph. i. 10,
where οἰκονομία seems to refer to *God's* dispensing of salvation, which was accomplished 'when the full time had come'.
See Mitton, *Eph.*, pp. 91–4, for a discussion of the word.

πληρῶσαι, in the sense of 'doing fully', 'carrying to completion', is illustrated by Rev. iii. 2, where 'deeds', ἔργα,
are spoken of as not πεπληρωμένα, not 'fully carried out';
and cf. Rom. xv. 19, Col. iv. 17. It is possible that here
there is the further implication that to proclaim the Gospel
is part of the *fulfilling* of God's plan.

26. τὸ μυστήριον. This word, which is of considerable
importance as a mirror of the distinctive qualities of

'revealed' religions, especially Christianity, has a curious history. It appears to be a true Greek word, and its prevailing sense in the classical period is a religious one—that of 'a secret rite' or an object connected with such a rite. Hence it came to be used (according to W. L. Knox, *Gentiles*, p. 183) for the secret meaning behind the rite—that of which the primitive rite came to be a symbol when it was interpreted theologically.

Accordingly, Judaism adopted it for the special sense of a divine secret, hitherto concealed but now revealed by God (Dan. ii. 28 f., 47 appears to be the first known instance), or concealed from the Gentiles but revealed to Israel: it became, for Judaism, a word associated with the self-revelation of God in history (cf. Tobit xii. 7 (‫א‬) μ. βασιλέως κρύπτειν καλόν, τὰ δὲ ἔργα τοῦ θεοῦ ἐξομολογεῖσθαι καὶ ἀνακαλύπτειν, cf. v. 11).[1]

The word may thus be supposed to have reached the N.T. charged with three associations:

　(i) An initiatory rite and its theological meaning.

　(ii) A divine secret, divulged by God.

　(iii) A secret, or something mysterious, generally.

Sense (ii) is easy to establish for the N.T., e.g. from our

---

[1] Further, it was transliterated into Hebrew letters as מִסְטֵירִין or מִסְתֵּירִין, *misṭerin* or *misterin*, and this, for the Jew, suggested מִסְתָּרִין or (in biblical Hebrew) מִסְתָּרִים, *mistarin* or *mistarim*, 'secrets' (W. L. Knox, *Gentiles*, pp. 227 f.)—a sense which the Greek μυστήριον had, indeed, itself already acquired in secular use. In the Greek O.T., μ. in Daniel represents רוּא or רָז, *raz* or *raza*, said to be a Persian loan-word = 'secret'. (*Raz* occurs also in the Dead Sea Scrolls, associated with apocalyptic ideas—not with Gnostic. See K. G. Kuhn, 'Die in Palästina gefundenen hebräischen Texte und das Neue Testament', in *Z.T.K.* XLVII (1950), pp. 204 f., and Bo Reicke, 'Traces of Gnosticism in the Dead Sea Scrolls?', in *J.N.T.S.* I, no. 2 (Nov. 1954), p. 138.) Otherwise it occurs in the LXX only in passages which are Greek in origin or for which there is no Hebrew extant, in Ecclus., Tobit, Judith, Wisdom, II Macc. In Dan. ii. 22, the Aramaic for 'secrets', מְסַתְּרָתָא, is not rendered by μυστήρια but by σκοτεινά (LXX) or ἀπόκρυφα (Theodotion).

present passage and from Rom. xvi. 25 and Eph. iii. 9; and indeed it is almost always 'found in connexion with words denoting revelation or publication; e.g. ἀποκαλύπτειν, ἀποκάλυψις...γνωρίζειν...φανεροῦν...λαλεῖν...λέγειν' (Lightfoot *in loc.*). So in II Thess. ii. 7 τὸ μ. τῆς ἀνομίας is a secret of wickedness destined to be revealed—a sort of blasphemous parody of the divine μ. (cf. *vv.* 8f.). In Ignatius *Ephes.* xix comes the famous paradox where the virginity of Mary, and her childbearing, and the death of the Lord are τρία μυστήρια κραυγῆς, 'three mysteries to be cried aloud' (Lightfoot). Sense (iii) is probably what is intended in certain other passages, e.g. I Cor. xv. 51, Rev. i. 20, xvii. 5, 7. An analogy to (i) may possibly be found in Eph. v. 32, where it may be that marriage is 'theologically' interpreted as of the relation between Christ and his Bride the Church.

But within the meaning (ii), which is the most characteristic of both Jewish and Christian 'revealed' religion, the Christians, of course, found Christ to be himself the centre of the μυστήριον: the incarnation summed up that divine secret which had been so long hidden but was now divulged. So in *v.* 27 here, and in ii. 2 below and (virtually) in I Cor. ii. 7. Cf., perhaps, Mark iv. 11. Robinson, *Eph.*, 'demonstrated that...in the New Testament it means, not something that must not be revealed to the uninitiated, but something that could not be known by men except by divine revelation but that, though once hidden, has now been revealed in Christ and is to be proclaimed so that all who have ears may hear it'. (C. E. B. Cranfield in *S.J.T.* v, no. 1 (Mar. 1952), p. 51.)

It is urged by some (e.g. Mitton, *Eph.*, p. 89) that in Ephesians, though not in Colossians, a further step is taken, and the μ., instead of being equated with Christ himself, is the inclusion of the Gentiles with the Jews in the Church, Eph. iii. 3–6. This is regarded as one of the points of differ-

ence between Ephesians and Colossians. But is not Col.
i. 26–9 intended in this sense? The μ. is 'that Christ is
among you (Gentiles)'—or (better still) the μ. is *both* Christ
himself *and* the fact that he is among them. See on ii. 2
below.

Besides the works cited above, see *T.W.N.T. s.v.* and
Masson, *Eph.*, p. 178, arguing that Ephesians and Colossians
are here essentially in agreement—but neither (at this point)
Pauline.

ἀπὸ τῶν αἰώνων.... Is ἀπό = '(concealed) from' or
'since'? Probably the latter, seeing that αἰών and γενεά are
not likely to be personified.

νῦν δὲ.... This anacoluthon is an intelligible one,
presenting no particular problem.

τοῖς ἁγίοις αὐτοῦ. See on *v.* 2 above.

27. τὸ πλοῦτος τῆς δόξης...ἡ ἐλπὶς τῆς δόξης. Δόξα is
one of those words which are charged with a new meaning
as a result of Hebrew–Christian religious experience. The
noun of δοκέω, it means, in Classical Greek, either *opinion* or
reputation. But in biblical use, the latter meaning, though
represented, has receded far into the background; while the
former has practically disappeared. Instead, the most
characteristic meaning of δόξα is *the glory of God*.

This is because δόξα was chosen by those who translated
the O.T. into Greek to represent the Hebrew כבוד—the
usual word for the splendour or glory of God. But they
filled it with more besides, for by their time the glory of
God had become closely associated with the famous
rabbinic word for the divine *presence*, or God's *act of dwelling*
among his people—*Shekinta* or *Shekina* (from שכן, to dwell).
This latter was properly represented by the Greek σκηνοῦν,
σκηνή; but God's indwelling was glorious, and δόξα became
so close a neighbour to (κατα)σκηνοῦν as sometimes to
overlap with it. δόξα became a comprehensive word for
God's glorious presence (cf. Rom. ix. 4).

It carried with it associations of *visible* light and splendour (as does 'brilliance' in its metaphorical sense); but, especially as the result of the Incarnation, the essential splendour came to be recognized as a *moral* splendour—the glorious life of service lived by Christ and laid down for others in the crucifixion; and although there were moments when this seemed to become visually bright (as at the Transfiguration or on the Damascus Road), radiance was recognized as a symbol for spiritual glory.

Consequently, St Paul can describe selfish and sensual persons as those whose δόξα—what they find most splendid, or what they revel in—is their disgraceful life (Phil. iii. 19); with the implication that a genuine Christian's δόξα is Christ, and a Christ-like life of service; and St John is at pains to show that the Shekina-glory of the life of Christ (John i. 14) is to be seen at its most brilliant when he is washing his disciples' feet (xiii. 1 ff.) or has reached the hour of death (xiii. 1); and he dramatically contrasts with this the ordinary, secular meaning of δόξα as *reputation, honour* (v. 44).

So far, then, as δόξα in a religious sense is applied to man, it means the glorious destiny designed by God for him (Rom. iii. 23, cf. Ps. viii). Without God, man is bound to fall short of it; but in Christ it is attained; and to be engaged in fulfilling such a destiny by suffering 'in Christ' is a glorious thing (Eph. iii. 13, cf. Rom. viii. 18, 21). But more often the word is applied to God, or Christ, or to some aspect of God's activity.

Thus, in our present passage, where the word occurs twice in quick succession, the 'wealth of glory' represented by the Incarnation, and, since then, by the presence of God in his Church through the Holy Spirit, is the ground for the Christians' 'confidence' (ἐλπίς) 'in a glorious destiny to come'. (See *T.W.N.T. s.v.* and A. M. Ramsey, *The Glory of God and the Transfiguration of Christ* (Longmans, 1949).)

ἐν ὑμῖν. The context (see on *v.* 26) seems to make 'among you' at least a very plausible alternative to 'within you'.

28. ... νουθετοῦντες πάντα ἄνθρωπον κ.τ.λ. The apostle's admonitions, teaching, and insight are here spoken of as directed towards 'offering' or 'presenting' each individual person to God as a mature Christian incorporated in Christ (see on *v.* 22 above, and cf. on ii. 10 below). In *v.* 22 above, παραστῆσαι may be a sacrificial term (see notes there). Here, the context seems to make the word more general—to 'bring' him into God's presence, or, possibly, to 'show him to be' a mature Christian, as a poet or dramatist 'represents' a character, 'exhibits' him as this or that (see L. and S., *s.v.*).

Commentators note that πάντα ἄνθρωπον may, like ἐν πάσῃ σοφίᾳ also (unless that describes the mode, not the content, of the instruction), be a deliberate rejoinder to some exclusive aspect of the false teachers' 'gospel'. There is no need to see in τέλειον an allusion to the 'initiation' (τελεόω) of mystery religions, though this is not impossible.

29. ἀγωνιζόμενος κατὰ τὴν ἐνέργειαν αὐτοῦ κ.τ.λ. To this striking and typically Christian combination of human effort and divine succour, an obvious parallel is Phil. ii. 12 f. But it runs right through the N.T.

ii. 1. ἡλίκον ἀγῶνα.... For the causes of this hard effort or contest (i.e. in prayer and thought and wrestling with anxiety), see Introduction, p. 27.

καὶ ὅσοι.... I.e., probably, 'and all the [others] who...'. In themselves, the words might mean 'even those who...', implying that there were many who, unlike these, were personally known to St Paul. But there is no evidence that St Paul had ever been in the Lycus valley, and if in i. 7 ἡμῶν is the right reading (see Introduction, p. 27) it is unlikely.

2. ἵνα κ.τ.λ. The end to which St Paul's labours are directed is described in terms reminiscent of the noble prayer of i. 9 ff.: that these Christians' hearts (i.e. their wills,

their spirits) may be encouraged or stiffened to boldness, that they may be welded together in love (συμβιβασθέντες being a nominative *ad sensum*, cf. iii. 16, Eph. iii. 17, iv. 2), and in such a way as to attain to the full wealth of conviction which spiritual insight brings—that is, to the perception of God's 'mystery', which is Christ.

τῆς πληροφορίας is probably descriptive of πλοῦτος—the wealth *consists* of conviction; and—

τῆς συνέσεως, qualifying the πληροφορία in its turn, may be a genitive of origin: the conviction is the result of insight, of understanding. And finally the whole goal is redefined comprehensively as ἐπίγνωσις (for which see on i. 9 and A Note on the Knowledge of God, p. 159) of God's 'mystery' which is Christ (see on i. 26).

τοῦ μυστηρίου τοῦ Θεοῦ, Χριστοῦ is probably the true reading (p⁴⁶ B Hil); and the spate of variants are either explanatory (τοῦ μ. τοῦ Θεοῦ, ὅ ἐστιν Χριστός) or are modifications of the sense (...τοῦ Θεοῦ Πατρὸς (τοῦ) Χριστοῦ, etc.). Thus 'Christ' is in apposition to 'God's mystery'—a striking sense. As in i. 27 above, the μυστήριον *is* Christ—but Christ in a particular aspect: there, in his universal aspect as among the Gentiles; here, as the embodiment of God's Wisdom.

3. ἐν ᾧ εἰσιν πάντες οἱ θησαυροὶ τῆς σοφίας κ.τ.λ. For σοφία and γνῶσις see on i. 9 and i. 15–23 above, and A Note on the Knowledge of God, p. 159. That in Christ are hidden away all (God's) stores of wisdom and knowledge, is an overwhelmingly impressive way of saying once more what has already been noted as implied by other phrases—namely, that Christ has become to Christians all that the Wisdom of God was, according to the Wisdom Literature, and more still. See on i. 19 above. There may also be a reference to secret, esoteric knowledge claimed by the false teachers: 'if there *is* a secret, it is all in Christ' is the apostle's reply.

Although οἱ θησαυροὶ τῆς σοφίας and ἀπόκρυφοι are printed as quotations by W.H. etc., the words are not found exactly in Isa. xlv. 3 καὶ δώσω σοι θησαυροὺς σκοτεινούς, ἀποκρύφους ἀοράτους ἀνοίξω σοι,..., to which the Bible Society's margin refers. Their other reference—to Prov. ii. 3f.—is suggestive enough, if the reader continues on through the succeeding verses. Windisch, *Weisheit*, adds Ecclus. i. 25 ἐν θησαυροῖς σοφίας παραβολαὶ ἐπιστήμης, βδέλυγμα δὲ ἁμαρτωλῷ θεοσέβεια.

ii. 4–iii. 4. *What I mean by saying that in Christ are included all possible stores of wisdom and insight amounts to this: nobody is to deceive you into thinking that something further is still needed, over and above incorporation in him. His death and resurrection were a decisive and final victory over all opposing forces; and if, when incorporated in him, you share that death and resurrection, you are not to submit to any arbitrary assertion that salvation is not complete without the addition of certain materialistic observances.*

This section contains (quite incidentally, and as a by-product of the argument) one of the most important of St Paul's descriptions of *what is achieved by the death of Christ*, and one of his most emphatic reiterations of the theme of *the incorporation of believers in Christ*. For the N.T. generally, and very clearly for St Paul, Christianity is more than a struggle to copy an example or follow a leader: it is 'death and resurrection'—death with Christ in the realm of all that is contrary to God's design, and resurrection with him into a new life in which we are free to obey the will of God. The drama of baptism provided a vivid background for these thoughts, as it made actual the condition to which they relate.

For further illustration of these themes, see:

(i) for the effect of Christ's death, Rom. v. 9, vi. 7, viii. 3, II Cor. v. 15;

(ii) for the incorporation of believers in Christ by baptism, Rom. vi. 3, 4; cf. II Cor. v. 14;

(iii) for the victory over the opposing forces, passages which may (after Masson on Col. ii. 14, 15) be classified into three types:

(*a*) the evil powers, though demonstrated by the resurrection of Christ to be in the wrong, are still potent as long as 'the present evil age' continues: Rom. vii. 7 ff., II Thess. ii, I Pet. v. 8f., I John v. 19, Rev. xii. 12;

(*b*) the evil powers are reconciled: Col. i. 20 (cf. *v.* 16);

(*c*) the evil powers have been vanquished: Col. ii. 15, I Pet. iii. 22, John xii. 31, 32, xvi. 11, 33, I John iii. 8.

Obviously, (*a*) and (*c*) are only different aspects of the same conviction, and, in any case, the power to *hurt* must be distinguished from the power to compel to *sin* (Rom. vi. 14 declares the latter already broken). But the really remarkable conception is (*b*). This is not easy to harmonize with (*a*) and (*c*); but it is not impossible to conceive of the vanquished being ultimately also reconciled. See note (vi) (*d*) on i. 15–23 and note on i. 20, above.

4. Commentators differ as to the paragraph divisions, and as to the meaning of τοῦτο λέγω ἵνα...; but it seems to make the most pointed sense if we start a new paragraph here, and if, instead of referring τοῦτο to what precedes (as, e.g., Theod. Mops. refers it to *v.* 1) and translating it 'I say this in order that...', we rather paraphrase thus: 'What I mean is, nobody is to talk you into error by specious words....' The so-called 'ecbatic' use of ἵνα, in an imperatival sense, is common enough; and for τοῦτο λέγω = 'what I mean is...', cf. I Cor. i. 12, Gal. iii. 17 (cf. iv. 1), and possibly Eph. iv. 17; also τοῦτο δέ φημι in I Cor. vii. 29 and perhaps in xv. 50; and τί οὖν φημι; in I Cor. x. 19. On the other hand, the γάρ in *v.* 5 is harder to justify on this showing: it will have to mean '...and you need not succumb, for I am helping...'. And if τοῦτο does refer *back*, then *v.* 5 picks up *v.* 1.

5. St Paul's belief in his spiritual presence with his

fellow-Christians at a distance, and theirs with him, was extremely vivid. See Phil. i. 7 and (most impressive) I Cor. v. 3–5.

τὴν τάξιν καὶ τὸ στερέωμα.... The fact that both these terms are found in military contexts makes it not unlikely that they are military metaphors here: 'your orderly formation and the firm front which your faith in Christ presents'. For τάξις see Xen. Anab. I. 2. 18, Plut. Vit. Pyrrh. xvi. 7. στερέωμα (which in the LXX often means the 'firmament' of heaven—the 'lid', as it were of wrought metal, which was believed to overarch the world) occurs in I Macc. ix. 14 in a military sense.

τῆς εἰς Χριστὸν πίστεως ὑμῶν: see on Philem. 5.

6, 7. The virtual identification of the tradition of the facts about Christ with the believer's experience of the living Christ himself is here strikingly illustrated: 'As, therefore, you received as tradition [the account of] Jesus as Christ and Lord, conduct your lives as incorporated in him.' The Christian Gospel is essentially an *historical* account of what happened in the past; yet also essentially, it means incorporation *now* in the still living Person of whom it tells— the contemporary Christ. Thus, in a sense, the living Christ is the tradition of himself. Cf. Eph. iv. 20f. and see O. Cullmann in *S.J.T.* III (1950), pp. 180ff.

6. τὸν Χριστὸν Ἰησοῦν τὸν Κύριον. The combination ὁ X. Ἰ. is found (though not in all MSS.) in Gal. v. 24, vi. 12, Eph. iii. 1 (all in genitive) and 11 (dative). Only here and in Eph. iii. 11 is it found with ὁ Κύριος added.

More often than not, St Paul uses Χριστός as all but a proper name (for a qualification, see on iii. 24). But in the present phrase, it is difficult not to give to τὸν X. (especially in view of the definite article) the force of a title, 'the Christ'. II Cor. iv. 5, Χριστὸν Ἰησοῦν Κύριον, is identical, except for the absence of articles; but there it is easy to take X. Ἰ. as a proper name, and translate K. '*as* Lord'.

'Jesus is Lord', or 'Jesus Christ is Lord', or 'Jesus is the Christ' were no doubt early 'creeds'; but our present phrase would then be a sort of double creed—'Jesus is the Christ and Lord'; hence its strangeness and unusualness.

ἐν αὐτῷ περιπατεῖτε: I.e. 'conduct your lives as incorporated in him' (see on i. 2). 'Walking' is a metaphor for conduct both in biblical and rabbinic Hebrew and in biblical Greek.

7. ἐρριζωμένοι κ.τ.λ. Their faith *has taken root* in Christ; they are therefore (with a change of metaphor and of tense) *being progressively built up* in union with him, and are *progressively reinforced* in their Christian conviction. It is possible, alternatively, to treat τῇ πίστει as instrumental rather than local, and as = *trust* in Christ rather than *conviction*.

8. συλαγωγῶν. This rare word occurs only in late writers. It probably means, not 'rob' or 'despoil' so much as 'kidnap', 'carry off bodily', as a slave raider does. It is a vividly pictorial expression for what is said in *v.* 4.

διὰ τῆς φιλοσοφίας καὶ κενῆς ἀπάτης. St Paul is placing the boasted wisdom of his opponents in a contemptuous light. This is no ground for belittling the intellect.

τὴν παράδοσιν τῶν ἀνθρώπων, man-made tradition, is to be contrasted with the true, living, divine 'tradition' just alluded to. St Paul is here combating some kind of traditional rules of a meticulous nature, just as Christ (Mark vii. 7, etc.) opposed the traditionalism of certain Palestinian Jews. I Pet. i. 18 refers to a 'tradition' which was possibly in existence in pagan circles outside Judaism (unless these pagans had first become proselyte Jews or 'God-fearers' before their conversion to Christianity: see van Unnik, *Verlossing*).

τὰ στοιχεῖα τοῦ κόσμου. Either 'rudimentary and worldly notions' or 'the elemental beings which control (or belong to) the world'. Basically, στοιχεῖα seems to mean 'component parts of a series' (cf. στείχειν, 'to go or progress', στίχος, στοῖχος, 'a row or line'); hence, the 'letters' which are the units of a line of writing; hence, 'elementary ABC'; hence, 'elements' in the physical sense; hence (according to the ideas of those days), 'the elemental powers', 'the stars', 'world or cosmic spirits'. Commentators and lexicographers adduce instances from Classical writers onwards for the meanings 'elementary teaching' and 'physical elements'; for the sense 'elemental beings' the evidence, apart from what may be deduced from the contexts of the word in the N.T., is later than Classical and, in all determinable cases, later than the N.T., and belongs to the astrological sorts of writing. In the N.T., the word is used in Heb. v. 12 of elementary teaching, and in II Pet. iii. 10 of the physical elements (?); otherwise, it occurs only here and in *v.* 20 below and in Gal. iv. 3, 9—all in connexion with a relapse from the freedom of Christianity into some dogmatic system (certainly a Judaistic one in the Galatian instance). Most commentators take it, in all its Pauline occurrences, as a reference to the elemental spirits; and Theod. Mops., among other ancient commentators, combined this with other meanings when he interpreted στοιχεῖα of the sun and moon *as controlling the ritual calendar.* Similarly Percy, *Probleme,* pp. 156ff. and Bornkamm, *Ende,* p. 148 combine two ideas when they explain the word as referring to the angels who, according to Jewish legend, *mediated the Law* (cf. Acts vii. 38, 53, Gal. iii. 19, iv. 9f.—which connects the στ. with the calendar observances—, Heb. ii. 2). Percy argues that, both in Galatians and Colossians, τὰ στοιχεῖα must be something *directly opposed* to Christ (not merely such elementary teaching as might provide a foundation for Christianity), and also something *sufficiently personal* to be regarded as holding people in subjection.

There is no reason to deny that a belief in demonic powers is natural in this context—see on *v.* 15 below, and cf. Eph.

vi. 10 ff. (where terms like κοσμοκράτορες can be paralleled
from astrological writings of later days); but, in view of the
absence of evidence outside the N.T. for any such sense of
στοιχεῖα until later times, it seems reasonable to take it
here to mean simply 'elementary teaching'—teaching by
Judaistic or pagan ritualists, a 'materialistic' teaching
bound up with 'this world' alone, and contrary to the freedom of the Spirit. H. St J. Thackeray also expressed himself against the 'demonic' interpretation (*The Relation of St
Paul to Contemporary Jewish Thought*, London, 1900); but
most modern commentators take the other view.

9. ἐν αὐτῷ κατοικεῖ κ.τ.λ. Here there is no doubt
(whatever the doubts in i. 19) that πᾶν τὸ πλήρωμα is the
subject of the verb. See on i. 19.

Θεότητος: commentators quote Bengel on Θεότης—
'non modo divinae virtutes' (that, says Lohmeyer, would
be θειότης, as in Rom. i. 20) 'sed ipsa divina natura'.
But what is the force of—

σωματικῶς? Commentators, ancient and modern, group
themselves, roughly speaking, round five interpretations:

(i) 'as an organized body'; i.e. the totality of the Godhead is 'not distributed through a hierarchy of beings'
(Dodd *in loc.*), but gathered into one 'organism' in Christ.
So H. R. Mackintosh, *The Person of Jesus Christ* (London,
1912), p. 73, says 'as a unity or in organic relation'. See
Abbott and Masson for the ancestry of this idea, which
seems to include the name of Chrysostom. Theod. Mops. also
comes near to it.

(ii) 'expressing itself through the Body [of Christ, i.e. the
Church]' (cf. the anonymous commentator in Chrysostom
in loc., cited by Lightfoot). So Robinson, *Eph.*, p. 88,
Masson, and Bornkamm, *Ende*, p. 145.

(iii) 'actually'—in concrete reality, not in mere seeming.
So Augustine, among others.

(iv) 'in essence'. So the Greek Fathers, and Calvin.

(v) 'assuming a bodily form', 'becoming incarnate'. So Lightfoot. Of these, (iv) seems highly improbable, if intelligible at all. Of the remainder,

(i) is attractive, especially if one of the mistaken notions current at Colossae was precisely that the divine attributes were distributed through a whole series of 'powers' which together comprised the πλήρωμα, and that Christ was only one among these many. But see p. 166 below for doubts attaching to this; and, in any case, a single adverb is a slender peg on which to hang so mighty a thought as the 'organization' in Christ of all these powers: would not some expansion of the phrase be necessary, such as συμβιβασθὲν εἰς ἓν σῶμα, μὴ διαμερισθὲν διὰ πολλῶν προσώπων?

(ii) has much to recommend it, especially in view of the words which immediately follow, suggesting that believers find their own completion only as incorporated in Christ. See Masson, who favours this; and Robinson, *The Body*, pp. 68f. The word κεφαλή in particular (v. 10) helps to make this interpretation acceptable; but (as before) σωματικῶς seems a strangely compressed and epigrammatic way of introducing so striking a thought, and one might have expected at least as much help as: ...σωματικῶς, τοῦτό ἐστιν ἐν τῷ αὐτοῦ σώματι, τῇ ἐκκλησίᾳ.

(iii) and (v) combined seem, on the whole, to present the fewest difficulties. This would presumably represent a certain element of polemic against 'docetism'—the error of treating the incarnation as though it were only *apparent*, not *actual* (cf., perhaps, v. 17 below). The chief objection to taking σωματικῶς thus, as representing a stress on the fact that the Godhead became really embodied, is the present tense, κατοικεῖ, which is not easy to treat as a reference to a past event in history (like John i. 14 σὰρξ ἐγένετο). Is it possible that it is used here as a Greek perfect tense is normally used—to represent the continuance in the present of some state begun in the past? It would then mean 'the

totality of deity lives in him—as it was embodied in him at
the incarnation '. See Lightfoot's lucid advocacy of the case
for (v), and his patristic references. See also J. Bonsirven,
Paul, pp. 61 f., for a discussion.

10. ἐστὲ ἐν αὐτῷ πεπληρωμένοι. Since the totality of the
divine attributes has its home in Christ, it is as incorporated
in him (in his Body the Church) that Christians find completeness. And if it is correct to see in the preceding
σωματικῶς a reference to the incarnation, then the
relevance of this sentence is all the more clear: human
beings, in this world, can dare to hope for 'completeness'
inasmuch as the divine πλήρωμα was actually seen incarnate.

In any case, the phrase is clearly an attack on the mistake
evidently current at Colossae, of supposing that 'completeness' could not be found through Christ alone, but must be
sought by additional religious rites and beliefs.

In a different mood, and in different words, much the
same thing occurs in Rom. viii. 32: 'He that spared not his
own Son, but delivered him up for us all, how shall he not
also with him freely give us all things (τὰ πάντα)?'

ἡ κεφαλή here probably denotes primarily supremacy: see
on i. 18 above.

11, 12. The main sense of these verses is clear: if it is asked
how this 'completeness', which has been brought within
human range by the incarnation, is appropriated, the answer
is that in Christian Baptism (a rite deeper and greater than
Jewish circumcision, whatever parallels may exist between
the two) the believer is identified, by faith, with Christ in
his obedient death and his triumphant resurrection.

But what is meant by ἐν τῇ ἀπεκδύσει τοῦ σώματος τῆς
σαρκός, ἐν τῇ περιτομῇ τοῦ Χριστοῦ? By itself, the first half
of the phrase would naturally mean 'in the stripping off of
the physical (literal) body'; but can this be reconciled with
the stress, in the context, on the non-physical nature of what
is meant—περιτομῇ ἀχειροποιήτῳ?

(i) It is tempting to take ἐν τῇ ἀπεκδύσει κ.τ.λ. as explanatory not of ἀχειροποιήτῳ but of an implied χειροποιήτῳ: '...not done by hands, i.e. *not* consisting in the stripping off of flesh from the body'—as though the Greek had been οὐ χειροποιήτῳ, τοῦτό ἐστιν οὐκ ἐν τῇ κ.τ.λ. (cf. Eph. ii. 11 τῆς λεγομένης περιτομῆς ἐν σαρκὶ χειροποιήτου). The chief objection to this ingenious interpretation (adopted by Moffatt in his translation, 1913) is that it really implies τῆς σαρκὸς τοῦ σώματος rather than τοῦ σώματος τῆς σαρκός.

(ii) Alternatively, then, τὸ σῶμα τῆς σαρκός might mean 'the personality as dominated by sensuality', a self-centred, sensual 'self'; and the stripping off of such a self, which is what happens in baptism, is aptly described as a spiritual counterpart of circumcision (cf. iii. 9 ἀπεκδυσάμενοι τὸν παλαιὸν ἄνθρωπον). For τῆς σαρκός='sensual' cf. ii. 18 ὁ νοῦς τῆς σ.; and for τὸ σῶμα with other qualifying genitives see Rom. vi. 6, vii. 24, Phil. iii. 21.

(iii) More daringly, Scott, *St Paul*, p. 36, takes it as referring to the death of Christ: when Christ stripped off his physical body he was, as it were, inaugurating that death to self in which the Christian, in baptism, is united with him. This has the distinct advantage of suiting well with the movement of thought in *v.* 15 (ἀπεκδυσάμενος κ.τ.λ. referring to Christ's triumphant death), and with the thought that runs through much of the N.T., that by suffering *physically* Christ embodied an obedience which is effective for all who are united with him: cf. Rom. vii. 4 ὑμεῖς ἐθανατώθητε τῷ νόμῳ διὰ τοῦ σώματος τοῦ Χριστοῦ, and I Pet. ii. 24 and iv. 1; and note the important ἐν τῷ σώματι τῆς σαρκὸς αὐτοῦ in Col. i. 22. The chief objection to this interpretation is precisely the absence of that αὐτοῦ in the present phrase; but conceivably the identification of the baptized with Christ is regarded as so close as to render a specifying pronoun out of place. It may be added that a further reason for the use of τοῦ σώματος τῆς σαρκός here, instead of simply τῆς σαρκός, may possibly be found in an implied contrast between the removal of a mere portion of flesh (as in literal circumcision) and the total surrender and death of Christ and, in him, of Christians. (See a useful discussion in Bieder.)

It will now be seen that the second half of the phrase, ἐν τῇ περιτομῇ τοῦ Χριστοῦ, may also be taken in two ways, analogous to (ii) and (iii) above: either 'with a Christian circumcision', i.e. a Christian and spiritual counterpart of literal circumcision; or 'in Christ's own circumcision', i.e. the death of Christ on the cross, which was, so to speak, his 'circumcision' on behalf of us all. (See Robinson, *The Body*, p. 46.)

(ii) above may be combined with either of these interpretations;

(iii) can best—if not only—go with the second.

The choice is thus between:

(*a*) 'when you stripped off your sensual nature, in a Christian "circumcision"';

(*b*) 'when you stripped off your sensual nature by (union with) Christ's own "circumcision" (i.e. his death)';

(*c*) 'when (Christ) stripped off his physical body, that is, in Christ's own "circumcision"'.

In view of i. 22 and *v.* 15 below, (*c*) seems, on the whole, the strongest claimant.

12. συνταφέντες αὐτῷ ἐν τῷ βαπτίσματι (*v.l.* βαπτισμῷ). Baptism in the N.T. is more often viewed as *death* than as *washing*. Christ's absolute obedience to the will of God—his whole-hearted filial acceptance of the Father's way—meant death; and it also meant resurrection: in that death and that life, God's laws were shown at work in their perfection. Similarly, a baptizand starts by whole-hearted acceptance of God's verdict on sin: he renounces sin, he 'dies to it', or (in the language of the Gospels, Mark viii. 34, etc.) he takes his position as a sentenced criminal carrying his own

gibbet out to the execution-ground; and only so is he united
to Christ also in a new quality of life. Faith (or trust) in the
God who raised Jesus from death is the means of apprehend-
ing this union in the sacrament. See Rom. vi. 1–11; and
note (with Masson) that Colossians and Ephesians alone
speak of the resurrection of believers as a *fait accompli*;
contrast the future tense of Rom. vi. 5.

13–15. The following interpretation starts by assuming
that God, not Christ, is consistently the subject of the verbs.
But this creates considerable difficulties, and the alternative
of admitting that Christ is the subject of at least some will
also be discussed.

13. ὑμᾶς. See Introduction, p. 27, n. 1.

τοῖς παραπτώμασιν καὶ τῇ ἀκροβυστίᾳ τῆς σαρκός. The
datives seem to be descriptive of circumstances (indeed,
p⁴⁶ and some other MSS. read ἐν); and the state of
literal uncircumcision seems to be alluded to as a *symbol* of
spiritual alienation from the covenants of God (cf. Eph.
ii. 11, 12). This is more probable than that τῆς σαρκός is
equivalent to an adjective = 'sensual' and defines uncircumcision as a moral, not literal, condition.

14. ἐξαλείψας τὸ καθ' ἡμῶν χειρόγραφον. A χειρόγραφον
is an 'IOU', a statement of indebtedness, personally signed
by the debtor. Philem. 19 is an example of the form: ἐγὼ
Παῦλος ἔγραψα τῇ ἐμῇ χειρί, ἐγὼ ἀποτίσω: it is a *signed
undertaking*. The bond in question here is signed by men's
consciences: for a Jew, it is his acceptance of the revealed
Law of God as an obligation to abide by; for the Gentile,
it is a corresponding recognition of obligation to what he
knows of the will of God. In either case, it is an 'auto-
graphed' undertaking: 'I owe God obedience to his will.
Signed, Mankind.' This χειρόγραφον is 'against us' because
we have manifestly failed to discharge its obligations—no
one felt this more keenly than Paul the Pharisee (cf. Rom.
vii. 16, 22, 23).

The dative τοῖς δόγμασιν is problematic. It is usually taken as descriptive or as depending on an implied γεγραμμένον —'consisting of, or written in terms of, decrees'; but it has to be admitted that such a construction seems to be unparalleled. The corresponding phrase in Eph. ii. 15 is relieved by the introduction of ἐν: τὸν νόμον τῶν ἐντολῶν ἐν δόγμασιν. Equally strained are the attempts to treat it as an instrumental or causal dative—'by means of the decrees' —and to attach it either to ἐξαλείψας ('having cancelled the bond by keeping God's decrees',—i.e. by means of obedience) or to ὑπεναντίον ἡμῖν ('opposed to us by means of or because of its adverse decrees'). The most attractive solution so far proposed is that of Robinson, *The Body*, p. 43, n. 1, namely, to treat the dative as implied in the action of the verb *to subscribe to* (behind χειρόγραφον): 'our subscription to the ordinances'. The Eph. version, if so, looks like a misunderstanding, or a rephrasing.

It is this debt, then, acknowledged by the conscience of man and proved against him by his own signature, that Christ, himself sinless, has acknowledged by becoming man, and discharged by accepting the death-warrant which the bond constituted. God (or Christ?) has cancelled the bond (literally 'smeared out', 'obliterated', as writing on wax was smoothed away) by removing it—in fact, says the daring metaphor, by nailing it to the cross: for the body of Christ, nailed to the cross, does in some sense represent humanity's guilt. Or is the metaphor that of the 'title' nailed over the criminal's head, indicating his crime? So Dibelius, but less convincingly. In any case, the metaphor is so violent as practically to rupture itself; but it opens a window into St Paul's thought about *how* Christ's death brings life to us. Another way of putting it is that, since Christ died and since we are dead with him by baptism 'into his death', therefore the 'IOU' is no longer valid: our death (with Christ) releases us from the obligation: see

Rom. vi. 7, vii. 6, Gal. ii. 19. A vivid connexion between the removal of sins and the cross of Christ is found also in I Pet. ii. 24.

προσηλώσας. This and John xx. 25 are the only N.T. references to nails at the crucifixion. There seems to be no evidence for the alleged custom of cancelling a bond by piercing it with a nail.

15. With ἀπεκδυσάμενος we are confronted by a problem of interpretation. If God and not Christ is the subject, it can hardly mean anything but 'stripping' in the sense of 'despoiling'—stripping a person of something that he is wearing; but if Christ is the subject, then it may mean 'stripping off from himself', 'divesting himself (of)'. Decision must wait until the end of the verse.

τὰς ἀρχὰς καὶ τὰς ἐξουσίας must here mean the supernatural powers believed to be dominating the world. In itself, it is true, the phrase need only refer to human 'authorities': Luke xii. 11 ὅταν δὲ εἰσφέρωσιν ὑμᾶς ἐπὶ τὰς συναγωγὰς καὶ τὰς ἀ. καὶ τὰς ἐ. (cf. xx. 20 παραδοῦναι αὐτὸν τῇ ἀ. καὶ τῇ ἐ. τοῦ ἡγεμόνος); Titus iii. 1 ἀρχαῖς ἐξουσίαις ὑποτάσσεσθαι; so (with ἐξουσίαι alone) Rom. xiii. 1. But several times in the Pauline letters the context demands that it be taken instead (or *as well*) in a supernatural sense: as well, if some scholars (as Cullmann, *C.T.*, pp. 191 ff.) are right when they argue for recognizing supernatural powers *simultaneously with* the human, acting through them and by their agency. See, besides the present passage, Rom. viii. 38 (ἀρχαί), Eph. i. 21, iii. 10, vi. 12 (ἀ. and ἐ.). Ambiguous are I Cor. xv. 24, Col. i. 16 (where it is just possible to argue that ἀ. and ἐ. represent τὰ ὁρατὰ ἐπὶ τῆς γῆς), ii. 10 (? = 'authority, wherever it may be'); and possibly I Cor. ii. 8 holds a demonic reference in οὐδεὶς τῶν ἀρχόντων τοῦ αἰῶνος τούτου (cf. John xiv. 30 ὁ τοῦ κόσμου ἄρχων, and Luke iv. 6). See also the combination of terms in I Pet. iii. 22, ἀγγέλων καὶ ἐξουσιῶν καὶ δυνάμεων. The super-

natural, demonic sense is to be found in Jewish or Jewish–
Christian apocalyptic writings—Testaments of the XII
Patriarchs, Levi iii. 8, Testament of Solomon xx. 15 (ed.
C. C. McCown, 1922, = Migne vol. cxxii, col. 1349), and
may be implied in some other passages which are not now
extant in Greek; but it is not found in the pagan Gnostic
writers (so Foerster in *T.W.N.T.* ii, 568).

ἐδειγμάτισεν ἐν παρρησίᾳ seems to mean 'displayed in
public boldly' (cf. Matt. i. 19, but *v.l.* παραδ.); and Lightfoot compares Horace, *Epist.* i. 17. 33 'captos ostendere
civibus hostes'.

θριαμβεύσας αὐτούς evidently means 'leading them (i.e.
the ἀρχαί and ἐξουσίαι—the masc. αὐτούς being a construction according to sense) as a victorious general leads
his prisoners in a triumphal procession'. θριαμβεύειν corresponds to Latin *triumphare*. In II Cor. ii. 14 it is used of
Christ leading Christians as (willing) captives (not 'causeth
us to triumph', as A. V.). But what of—

ἐν αὐτῷ? If (as has been assumed up to now) God is still
the subject of the verbs, then ἐν αὐτῷ probably means 'in
Christ' or 'by means of him' (cf. σὺν αὐτῷ in *v.* 13 above).
It could, however (even retaining God as subject), be
referred to the cross of Christ—'leading them in triumph by
means of the cross' (cf. Eph. ii. 16, where ἐν αὐτῷ, 'by it', is
so used).

More dramatic still is to take Christ as the subject of
θριαμβεύσας, and ἐν as local rather than instrumental:
'leading them in triumphal procession upon the cross', as a
victorious conqueror led his captives behind the chariot in
which he rode.

Looking back over the passage 13–15, it is undoubtedly
natural to take God as the subject of συνεζωοποίησεν in
v. 13 (see *v.* 12); but from ἐξαλείψας or ἦρκεν (*v.* 14) onwards, Christ seems to be the more natural subject. Perhaps
we must acknowledge an illogical transition from the one

to the other in the course of this section. This is in keeping
with that identification between the activity of God and
the activity of Christ which is a familiar feature of N.T.
thought.

Returning, then, to the ἀπεκδυσάμενος of *v.* 15, the
sense 'despoiling', stripping the opposing powers of their
strength, would fit, whether God or Christ were subject
(and it matches the metaphor in θριαμβεύσας); but it is
questionable whether this verb could be so used in the
middle voice (Lightfoot regards it as impossible and, in any
case, contrary to the use of this particular verb elsewhere;
and more recent authorities can find no exact parallels: see
D.-B., §316. 1). It seems better, therefore, to accept that
Christ is the subject, and to translate it 'divesting himself'.

But divesting himself of what? Either of his flesh or of
the opposing powers. Robinson, *The Body*, p. 41, argues for
the former (which is also 'the common interpretation of the
Latin fathers'—Lightfoot): 'It is through the σάρξ that
death and its forces have control over human nature. The
dying Jesus, like a king, divests Himself of that flesh, the
tool and medium of their power, and thereby exposes them
to ridicule for their Pyrrhic victory.' On this showing, τὰς
ἀρχὰς κ.τ.λ. is governed by ἐδειγμάτισεν alone, not also by
ἀπεκδυσάμενος. Lightfoot favours the alternative ('the
common interpretation of the Greek fathers'): 'The powers
of evil, which had clung like a Nessus robe [a reference to
the legend of Hercules and the fatal robe poisoned by the
blood of the centaur Nessus] about His humanity, were torn
off and cast aside for ever.' Scott, *St Paul*, pp. 34 ff., combines the two; for, though apparently accepting 'He
stripped off from Himself the Principalities and Powers', he
also paraphrases: 'He divested Himself of that flesh, the
medium through which He had become involved in the
human experience of the hostility of the evil Potentates and
Powers.' The absence of τὴν σάρκα and the order of the

words favour interpreting as Lightfoot. But nowhere else is ἀπεκδύσασθαι used in so daringly metaphorical a way; and in any case there is no doubt that, for St Paul, 'divesting himself of his flesh' (the less daring metaphor) would have amounted to the same thing. See on *vv.* 11 f. above; and, especially, iii. 8f. below and note on iii. 5–17.

It is possible (so Lightfoot) that Zech. iii. 1 ff.—the symbolical vision of the High Priest divested of filthy garments and splendidly reinvested—lies behind the thought.

ἀπέκδυσις (ii. 11) and ἀπεκδύσασθαι (ii. 15, iii. 9) do not occur in the parallel passage in Ephesians, nor anywhere else in the N.T.; and Eph. ii. 14–16 differs also in that the achievement of Christ on the cross is related specifically to the reconciliation of Jew and Gentile, which is not the case with Col. ii. 15, unless (with Percy, *Probleme*, pp. 92 ff.) we take the ἀρχαί and ἐξουσίαι to be the forces behind Jewish legalism.

The following paraphrase may now be offered of *vv.* 14 f.: 'Deleting the adverse bond signed by us as committing us to the decrees of law—the bond which was opposed to us— he has removed it, nailing it to the cross. Divesting himself of the rulers and authorities, he boldly displayed them, leading them in triumphal procession on the cross.'

16ff. In this case (so the argument continues), if the powers controlling the material world have been so signally defeated by the death of Christ, there is no reason for submitting to a materialistic and merely external ritual (such as seems to have been declared essential by the false teachers).

16. For further references to scruples among Christians about eating and drinking, see Rom. xiv. 1 ff. (an especially close parallel to this verse), I Tim. iv. 2, 3, Titus i. 14 f., Heb. ix. 10, xiii. 9. I Cor. viii presents a rather different problem.

17. ἅ ἐστιν σκιὰ τῶν μελλόντων, τὸ δὲ σῶμα τοῦ Χριστοῦ: 'which (material symbols implied by *v.* 16) are only a shadow of what was to come, whereas the substance belongs (understand ἐστιν) to Christ.' For the contrast σκιά–σῶμα, commentators can cite Josephus *B.J.* ii. 28 and Philo *de Conf.* 190; and Heb. x. 1 (σκιὰν...οὐκ αὐτὴν τὴν εἰκόνα τῶν πραγμάτων) is a close parallel to the thought—a thought which is not so characteristic of the Pauline writings as of Hebrews.

But if σῶμα thus means, in this passage, primarily 'substance', 'reality' as opposed to insubstantial shadow, yet it is possible that τὸ σῶμα τοῦ Χριστοῦ carried with it further associations also, and that it suggested the Church, in whose fellowship all the great 'realities' were found—pardon, sanctification, communion with God, etc. (see Masson *in loc.*)—of which ritual, whether Jewish or non-Jewish, was only a shadow. Moreover, it probably suggested that famous verse which, in the prevalent LXX version of Ps. xl. 7, read (as quoted in Heb. x. 5) θυσίαν καὶ προσφορὰν οὐκ ἠθέλησας, σῶμα δὲ κατηρτίσω μοι: Christ's body, offered in sacrifice, was the reality to which the mere 'shadow'—the sacrificial system—pointed. Thus 'substance', 'Church', and 'final, perfect sacrifice' may all be ideas which would have crowded into the listeners' minds when this phrase in our letter was read, or at any rate into the writer's mind when it was written.

18 is crowded with problems of interpretation:

καταβραβευέτω seems, to judge from the scanty occurrences quoted (e.g.) by L. and S., M.M. *s.v.* and Stauffer in *T.W.N.T. s.v.* βραβεύω, and by Percy (*Probleme*, pp. 143–146), to mean either 'give an adverse decision' against someone, or 'deprive of his rightful prize' (βραβεῖον, see Phil. iii. 14). Jerome's paraphrase, *nemo adversum vos bravium accipiat* (*Epist.* cxxi *ad Algas*, 879), presumably means 'win the prize over your heads' or 'to your detriment', and so does Theod. Mops.', *nemo bravium vestrum tollat*; but (judging by its etymology) the verb might well mean 'decide (as an umpire) against you'—i.e. 'declare you disqualified', and this would apply remarkably well to a situation (cf. κρινέτω, v. 16) in which the theosophic ritualist declares the Pauline believer to be no genuine competitor in the race at all. See Field, *Otium*, pp. 120ff.

θέλων ἐν κ.τ.λ. It seems best to take this as a barbarism derived from the Semitic idiom of the LXX, where θέλειν ἐν is sometimes used for 'ב חפץ, 'to delight in'. For θέλειν = 'like', cf. Luke xx. 46 τῶν θελόντων περιπατεῖν ἐν στολαῖς ....The compound ἐθελοθρησκία in v. 23 points to a similar use of ἐθελο-.

The alternative—to join θέλων to καταβραβευέτω and translate 'disqualify you with relish', taking ἐν as instrumental, 'by means of',—seems much less likely.

ταπεινοφροσύνῃ, 'humiliation', 'humility' is a technical term for 'fasting' in Hermas *V.* III. 10. 6, *S.* v. 3. 7 (so Dibelius); and cf. the verb of fasting in Lev. xxiii. 29, Ezra (LXX II Esdras) viii. 21. This fits the present context well, and is supported by the addition, in v. 23, ἀφειδίᾳ σώματος. In iii. 12 below, on the contrary, it is brought into a fully Christian context, as a quality and a virtue, not a practice.

ἃ ἑόρακεν ἐμβατεύων. ἃ ἑόρακεν is generally taken as = ὁράματα, 'visions': the false teacher claims mystical insight, alluding to 'the things he has seen'; and the strictures on him here are reminiscent of the tirades against the false prophets with their deceiving visions in Jer. xxiii. 25ff. (cf. also the ἐνυπνιαζόμενοι of Jude 8). In the Fourth Gospel, Jesus is represented as himself using the phrase: iii. 11 ὃ ἑωράκαμεν μαρτυροῦμεν, viii. 38 ἃ ἐγὼ ἑώρακα παρὰ τῷ Πατρὶ λαλῶ; and commentators quote Rev. i. 2 ὅσα εἶδεν. (Note that many MSS. insert a negative—μή or οὐ— 'what he has not seen' (cf. Ezek. xiii. 3); but there is weighty evidence against it.)

What, then, is ἐμβατεύων, governing 'what he has seen'? There seem to be three main possibilities:

(i) It is a term borrowed from the mystery religions, and refers to entering the sanctuary after initiation. In inscriptions belonging to the sanctuary of Apollo at Claros (perhaps second century A.D., Dibelius), it is found in conjunction with μυεῖσθαι and παραλαμβάνειν τὰ μυστήρια. Presumably it would have to mean here that, as an initiate into the shrine, so the Colossian 'penetrates' into the visions he claims to see. But '...in the inscriptions ἐμβατεύειν is always the sequel of μυεῖσθαι and not part of it' (A. D. Nock in *J.B.L.* LII (1933), criticizing Dibelius); and the use of ἐμβατεύειν with the *visions*, not the *shrine*, as the object seems far-fetched and inappropriate, especially since the tense of ἑόρακεν would produce the meaning 'penetrating into visions he has already seen'! (See Preisker in *T.W.N.T. s.v.*)

(ii) It is an O.T. metaphor from the occupation of the promised land: Josh. xix. 49, etc. M.M. *s.v.* show that this sense (in respect of property) is attested also by the papyri. This is just conceivable: the person treats his visions as his most prized territory, his very Mecca. But again, how far-fetched!

(iii) It means 'investigating'. For this sense are adduced II Macc. ii. 30 (without an object, = 'enter into details', A. D. Nock, *loc. cit.*), Philo, *de Plant.* 80 (*v.ll.* ἐμβαθοῦντες, ἐμβαθύνοντες), and (according to Percy, *Probleme*, p. 170) Chrysostom and Athanasius. Preisker (*loc. cit.*) argues for this: instead of holding the truth once for all in Christ, the false teachers are forever investigating (cf., perhaps, II Tim. iii. 7). But this is very tame, where the context seems to require something more assertive.

More acceptable, were it admissible, would be R.V. *mg.*, 'taking his stand upon'; but there appears to be no evidence for this meaning. It is not surprising that corruption has been suspected (though, if so, it must be very early, since existing MSS. show no trace of it), and emendations offered.

Lightfoot proposed ἐώρᾳ (or αἰώρᾳ) κενεμβατεύων, 'treading the empty air in a state of suspension' (for so he apparently intended it). C. Taylor, more simply, had offered ἀέρα κενεμβατεύων, 'treading the empty air' (*Journ. of Philol.* vol. VII (1877), no. 13, pp. 130 ff., cited (with wrong date) by Hort, W.H. II, p. 127). Perhaps there is an even better case to be made for an emendation such as ἃ ἑόρακεν (or the shortened form ἑώρα) κενεμβατεύων, 'walking upon the insubstantial ground of his visions' (like Socrates in the *Clouds* of Aristophanes l. 225, who says ἀεροβατῶ). Alexander More (*ad quaedam loca Novi Foederis Notae*, Paris, 1668) alludes to the possibility of reading ἃ μὴ (sic) ἑώρακεν[1] κενεμβατεύων, though he prefers to retain ἐμβατεύων, taking it with the εἰκῇ which follows so as to make it practically equivalent in meaning to κενεμβατεύων. Curcellaeus (H. Wetstein, Amsterdam, 1711) has κενεμβατεύειν (sic). Hitzig (in Nestle's apparatus) suggested τὰ μετέωρα κενεμβατεύων. L. and S. do not recognize the word κενεμβατεύων, but κενεμβατεῖν is well attested.

Thus, we must either take our choice of doubtful conjectural emendations, or make the best we can of the existing text.

τοῦ νοὸς τῆς σαρκὸς αὐτοῦ: an impossible phrase if taken literally—'his physical mind'—but evidently meaning 'his materialistic or sensual outlook'. What so inflates the person with senseless pride is the value which he selfishly sets upon the merely external, material symbols and observances. See on vv. 11 f. above (note (ii)).

19. τὴν Κεφαλήν. See on i. 18.

ἐξ οὗ is constructed according to sense: ἡ Κεφαλή becomes masculine because it is Christ.

ἁφῶν καὶ συνδέσμων. Lightfoot gives ample evidence for the anatomical use of these words. ἁφαί are, strictly, points of contact (ἅπτομαι), and so, virtually, 'joints' ('provided that we use the word accurately of the relations between

---

[1] ἑόρακεν, as in most texts, is simply an alternative spelling.

contiguous limbs, and not loosely...of the parts of the limbs themselves in the neighbourhood of the contact'—Lightfoot). σύνδεσμοι are the bands by which the body is held together, and, in particular, 'ligaments' (but below, iii. 14, in a probably different sense). Whether one should press the question what they correspond to in the Church is another matter. Masson (on Eph. iv. 1–16) makes them Ministers, as distinct from ordinary members, and sees in this a difference from the authentic Pauline outlook.

ἐπιχορηγούμενον. Robinson, *Eph.* (on Eph. iv. 16 διὰ πάσης ἀφῆς τῆς ἐπιχορηγίας), argues for the meaning 'furnished', 'equipped'. The whole phrase, if so, would mean: '...the whole body, equipped and bonded together with joints and ligaments, grows as God intends it to grow' (lit. 'grows the growth of God'). Lightfoot, like many others, preferred to take ἐπιχορηγούμενον as 'supplied', and διὰ τῶν ἀ. καὶ συνδ. as indicating the channels of supply. True, joints and ligaments are not, in fact, such channels; and the Ephesians passage is possibly easier to construe in Robinson's way. But ἐπιχορηγούμενον διὰ...is odd Greek for 'equipped *with*', and it seems better to accept loose physiology and translate '...the whole body, supplied and bonded together by joints and ligaments...'. Masson, *Eph.* p. 196, returns to this interpretation despite a different view in his (earlier) Colossians.

20. Εἰ ἀπεθάνετε κ.τ.λ. Those who take στοιχεῖα as = 'elemental spirits' (see on *v.* 8) can give extra point here to the idea of dying with Christ 'from out of' (ἀπό) their control (especially if they are angels who mediate the Law). But Christ's death, equally, has put an end to control by elementary notions of materialism.

21. If there is anything more than a rhetorical distinction between ἅψῃ and θίγῃς, it is the *first* (as commentators point out) which is nearer to 'handle' and the *second* to 'touch'— the reverse of the A.V.; see the alteration in the R.V.

22. ἅ.... The antecedent is evidently the material things with which the rules 'handle not', etc., are concerned.

εἰς φθορὰν τῇ ἀποχρήσει seems to mean 'destined to perish in the course of using them up'.

τὰ ἐντάλματα...ἀνθρώπων is from (or at least is a reminiscence of) Isa. xxix. 13, which had played a part in controversies of this sort since the days of Jesus himself: Matt. xv. 9, cf. Tit. i. 14.

23. This verse is by common consent regarded as hopelessly obscure—either owing to corruption or because we have lost the clue. Perhaps the best that can be made of it is something like this: 'which (rules about diet, etc.) have indeed a reputation for wisdom, with their voluntary delight in religiousness and self-mortification and severity to the body, but are of no value in combating sensual indulgence'.

This involves the following assumptions:

(i) λόγος = 'reputation', 'credit'. Lightfoot, in his masterly analysis of the possibilities, makes a reasonably good case for this. In a suggestively related, though not identical, sense (that of 'reasonableness'), note Acts xviii. 14 and (from Wettstein) Demosthenes, c. Leptinem 162: ἔστι δὲ τοῦτο, οὕτως μὲν ἀκοῦσαι, λόγον τινὰ ἔχον. εἰ δέ τις αὐτὸ ἀκριβῶς ἐξετάσειε, ψεῦδος ἂν φανείη. Cf. εὔλογος.

(ii) οὐκ introduces an adversative clause, as though it were ἀλλὰ οὐκ, and answers to the preceding μέν. II Tim. ii. 14 may be compared for a similar abruptness, though there, admittedly, it is not a matter of an adversative particle lacking: μὴ λογομαχεῖν, ἐπ' οὐδὲν χρήσιμον, ἐπὶ καταστροφῇ τῶν ἀκουόντων.

(iii) ἐν τιμῇ τινι πρός = 'of any value against' (i.e. in combating). This is the most questionable part of the interpretation, but again Lightfoot produces considerable support for ἐν τιμῇ and πρός in the required senses. (Note also I Pet. ii. 7, ὑμῖν οὖν ἡ τιμή....)

Suggested alternatives include:

(i) Taking οὐκ ἐν τιμῇ τινι πρὸς κ.τ.λ. as = '(the body) treated with no respect in regard to satisfying its desires'. This involves the extreme difficulties of linking the phrase awkwardly to ἀφειδίᾳ σώματος and interpreting it as a further description of the Colossians' ascetical practices; and of taking πλησμονὴ τῆς σαρκός in the sense of 'legitimate bodily satisfaction';

(ii) Taking πρὸς πλησμονὴν κ.τ.λ. as an adversative addition: '...practices which are of no value, but only tend to sensual indulgence' (for which again cf. II Tim. ii. 14).

(iii) Bornkamm, *Ende*, pp. 151 f., remarks a love of five-fold expressions in Iranian Gnosticism, and suggests that the writer may be deliberately falling in with this in iii. 5 (five vices) and 8 (five evil practices) and 12 (five virtues, with ἀγάπη added to hold all together); and, if so, why not find the clue to the present passage in a five-fold scheme? The Colossian error taught, perhaps, that (*a*) *voluntary initiation* (ἐθελοθρησκία) brought with it the duties of (*b*) ταπεινο-φροσύνη and (*c*) ἀφειδία τοῦ σώματος; and that would (*d*) bring them *honour* (τιμή)—that is, according to the mysteries, *deification* (which St Paul denies—οὐκ ἐν τιμῇ τινι) and (*e*) *fulness*—the condition of being filled with the divine power—(which St Paul sarcastically parodies by πλησμονὴν τῆς σαρκός: the only 'fulness' to which it leads is one of sensuality).

(iv) Dibelius favours taking as the main sentence ἅ ἐστιν πάντα εἰς φθορὰν τῇ ἀποχρήσει, οὐκ ἐν τιμῇ τινι πρὸς πλησμονὴν τῆς σαρκός (i.e. 'which are all destined to perish, and not to receive any honour...'), and treating κατὰ τὰ ἐντάλματα ...σώματος as a parenthesis expressing St Paul's criticism of the dictatorial rules of mere men.

Of these, (iii) is ingenious but far-fetched (see a critique in Dibelius); in (iv) it is difficult to see what to do with πρὸς πλησμονὴν τῆς σαρκός; and (i) and (ii) both seem strained and awkward. On the whole, then, they all compare unfavourably with the suggestion with which this note began, which is ably defended by Lightfoot, and (until further light comes) must stand for the time being. It is represented by the R.V.

It is worth adding that according to Philo (*de Vit. Contempl.* 35 and 37, quoted by Lightfoot) the Therapeutae, an ascetic Jewish sect in Egypt, comparable to the Essenes in Palestine, delighted in σοφία, which is associated with δόγματα, and abhorred πλησμονή. This suits well with the above interpretation which implies that the Colossian rules were meant to combat πλησμονή.

iii. 1–4 represents the positive counterpart to ii. 20–23: Christians have not only died with Christ but also risen with him.

This passage contains the only explicit reference in this epistle to a future coming or revealing of Christ. It is customary, in discussing N.T. teaching, to distinguish between 'realized eschatology' and 'futurist eschatology'— that is, between, on the one hand, a presentation of the Nativity, Ministry, Death, and Resurrection of Christ as the 'final' or 'absolute' or 'unique' work of God already achieved or already initiated; and, on the other hand, a presentation of 'finality' as still to be realized, or at any rate revealed, in the future. The one stresses the transcendent newness and uniqueness of what has already been done; the other stresses the transitory and incomplete nature of the present era, and the fact that the ultimate reality is still concealed. So far as any one writer can be attached to one side more than the other, the Fourth Gospel is most obviously the writing of 'realized eschatology', with its stress on Jesus as the eternal Word of God, and its phrases about the believer having already passed from death to life. On the whole, St Paul allows more weight than the Fourth Evangelist to futurist phrases. But in fact both writers contain both elements (even if in different proportions); and here, at any rate, is a very striking paradoxical combination of the two: the Christian has, in a sense, already gone past the last day, the day of judgment; already dead with Christ, he has already been raised again with him (see on ii. 12 above): he already lives on a new level. But nevertheless, it yet remains for that new life to be actually manifested: at present it is concealed, at least from the worldly—perhaps, in a measure, from the believer himself: 'the world' (says Bengel, quoted by Lightfoot) 'knows neither Christ nor the Christians; and not even the Christians themselves fully know themselves'. But in the open manifestation and establishment of Christ's triumph, Christians too will be openly seen, sharing it with him. Cf. I John iii. 2; also I Thess. iv. 13–18 and I Cor. xv. 51–4. A study of verbs compounded with συν- in the N.T. throws important light on the meaning of this close connexion between the life of Christians and the life of Christ.

iii. 1, 2. τὰ ἄνω ζητεῖτε...τὰ ἄνω φρονεῖτε. φρονεῖν, φρόνημα are important words in the N.T. vocabulary of religious experience and response. The phrases here evidently refer to a concern for matters which are 'above' in the sense of ultimately essential, transcendent, belonging to God, as contrasted with matters which are 'below'—concerned, that is, with a trivial or a selfish view of life. Both in the Fourth Gospel and in the Pauline writings, this anti-thesis between ἄνω and κάτω (or ἐπὶ τῆς γῆς) is employed: cf. Phil. iii. 19, 20, and ἡ ἄνω Ἰερουσαλήμ in Gal. iv. 26. It is a vivid way of contrasting 'spiritual' with 'unspiritual' ways. But the N.T. carefully guards against imagining that *matter*, as such, or this life on earth, as such, is evil: it is the trivial and selfish *use* of it which is essentially τὸ κάτω. Indeed, it is precisely baptism into Christ (a sacrament of the *incarnate* Lord) which delivers a man from regarding matter in itself as the great enemy (see Lightfoot *in loc.*);

NOTES [iii. 1–4

and St Paul clearly believed in the use of material things
so as to transform personal relationships (see I Cor. x, xi):
he was anything but opposed to the sacramental use of
matter, or indifferent to the Church's responsibilities to its
environment. What he does attack is an unspiritual and
materialistic type of superstitious ritualism: cf. Gal. iii. 1–6.

Note that Christ's resurrection and glorification are mentioned together. It is not clear that St Paul distinguished
them in the way in which they are distinguished pictorially
in Acts i. 1–9.

3. κέκρυπται. This is sometimes taken to mean that the
new life of Christians in Christ is a secret to the unregenerate
(and in part even to themselves). Until the End, it remains
unrevealed. But is there not rather some connexion with the
ἀπόκρυφοι of ii. 3? Christ is the storehouse of all God's secrets,
including the Church's new life. Also (Dr Dodd suggests to
me) there may be allusion to the pagan idea that death
means that a man is 'hidden' in the earth—dead and done
with: Christians claim that they are hidden indeed—but in
Christ.

4. ὁ Χριστός...ἡ ζωὴ ἡμῶν. For the textual problem
(ἡμῶν B *al* sy *ς*; ὑμῶν p⁴⁶ ℵ DG *pm* lat arm), see Introduction, p. 27, n. 1. The phrase expresses epigrammatically that
identification of the life of Christians with the life of Christ
which runs through St Paul's references to his own experience; cf. Phil. i. 21 ἐμοὶ γὰρ τὸ ζῆν Χριστός (though
here, admittedly, τὸ ζῆν is occasioned by the contrast with
τὸ ἀποθανεῖν), Gal. ii. 20 ζῶ δὲ οὐκέτι ἐγώ, ζῇ δὲ ἐν ἐμοὶ
Χριστός κ.τ.λ. A striking form of the same thought is the
infinitive idiom affected by Ignatius of Antioch: *Ephes.* iii
Ἰησοῦς Χριστός, τὸ ἀδιάκριτον ἡμῶν ζῆν ('our inseparable
life'), xi τὸ ἀληθινὸν ζῆν (so also *Smyrn.* iv, and cf. *Trall.*
ix), *Magn.* i Ἰησοῦ Χριστοῦ τοῦ διὰ παντὸς ἡμῶν ζῆν.

σὺν αὐτῷ. George, *Communion*, pp. 154f., points out that
St Paul does not, except in this epistle, make much use of

112

σύν; and that the actual state of *being* with the Lord is referred only to the *future* (Phil. i. 23 and I Thess. iv. 17), although there are other verbs compounded with σύν which relate to past experiences. Dodd, *F.G.*, p. 193, points out that even in this phrase Paul does not (like the Fourth Evangelist) speak expressly of Christ as *in God*. See on i. 2, above.

iii. 5–17. *This paragraph marks the transition from what is primarily theology to the application of this doctrinal matter to life and conduct.*

It is characteristic of the Pauline letters generally that they fall thus into two parts (think, for instance, of the transition at Rom. xii); and in this respect they contrast with epistles such as Hebrews and I Peter, with their interwoven and alternating doctrine and exhortation. Yet, even in the Paulines, the division is far from rigid; indeed, Christianity is such that its 'theology and ethics' are, by their very nature, inseparable; for it is neither a merely intellectual statement of philosophy nor merely a system of rules for conduct: it is incorporation in Christ, which means faith and practice in one—pattern and power together; mind, will, and emotions working in co-operation. It is in keeping with this that the *doctrinal indicative*, stating a fact ('you have died with Christ...', ii. 20), is followed by the *ethical* or *moral imperative* ('Therefore put to death...', iii. 5).

Recent research (associated for readers of English especially with the names of Archbishop Philip Carrington and Dr E. G. Selwyn) has shown reason for believing that, before any of our known Christian writings took shape, there was already a recognized body of teaching delivered to enquirers who were seeking Baptism; and the various 'headings', so to speak, of such teaching seem to appear (sometimes, significantly, in the same order and with the same catchwords) in independent writings. The present paragraph and what follows it may usefully be compared in this respect with other parts of the N.T. For details, see Dr Carrington's *The Primitive Christian Catechism* (Cambridge, 1940), and Dr E. G. Selwyn's discussion in his commentary on I Peter (Macmillan, 1946), Essay II. Meanwhile note the 'headings' to the various clauses in the homily: *v.* 5 νεκρώσατε, *v.* 9 ἀπεκδυσάμενοι, *vv.* 10, 12 καὶ ἐνδυσάμενοι, ἐνδύσασθε; and observe that νεκρώσατε and ἀπεκδυσάμενοι are irresistibly reminiscent of the description in ii. 14 f. of the death of Christ and of his ἀπέκδυσις. Nothing is clearer than that Baptism and entry upon the Christian life meant, for St Paul, so close a connexion between the believer and Christ (in his Body the Church) that Christ's death (his 'stripping') and his 'reclothing' became also the believers'. See on ii. 11, 12, iii. 4 above. This particular language—that of divesting and reinvesting—was no doubt dramatically symbolized by the baptizand's unclothing before immersion and reclothing after it. *Thus, Christian conduct is the result, not simply of the effort to be good, but of incorporation into the Body of Christ.*

5. Νεκρώσατε. Cf. Rom. viii. 13 θανατοῦτε. The Latin-English equivalent, 'mortify', has acquired, in its long history, certain associations, which are alien to St Paul's meaning: 'mortification of the flesh' often stands for self-inflicted bodily pain, as by flagellation, practised by ascetics; or, more generally, for 'self-denial' in the form of abstaining from what one enjoys, with a view either to gaining control over the body[1] or (misguidedly) to acquiring merit. But St Paul's meaning is evidently something like what Christ dramatically expressed by 'Take up your cross and follow me' (Mark viii. 34, etc.): that is, to follow Jesus means complete devotion, even to the extent of regarding oneself—

[1] If there is a Pauline passage nearer to this sense of mortification, it is I Cor. ix. 26 f., where the theme is gaining control of the body.

one's own private desires and ambitions—as 'sentenced to death', or as in fact 'dead'. Yet there is a difference; for whereas Jesus, during his ministry and before his death and resurrection, could only summon disciples to the effort to 'follow' in obedience, St Paul, called by the risen, heavenly Christ, has found, by incorporation in him, the transforming strength to achieve such devotion. The injunction νεκρώσατε —kill self-centredness—becomes progressively a possibility for those who are united by Baptism with the Body of Christ. Compare, then, the following phrases: Rom. vi. 4 'we were buried...with him through baptism into death'; v. 11 '...reckon ye also yourselves to be dead unto sin...'; Gal. ii. 20 'I have been crucified with Christ...'; and, in this epistle, ii. 20, iii. 3 above. An illuminating parallel to St Paul's phrase in Rom. vi. 11 is I Pet. iv. 1 'Forasmuch then as Christ suffered in the flesh, arm yourselves also with the same mind' (τὴν αὐτὴν ἔννοιαν ὁπλίσασθε).

Thus, 'mortification' in such a context evidently means transformation of the will, a metamorphosis of one's whole attitude, a radical shifting of the very centre of the personality from self to Christ, such that 'death' to selfishness is by no means too strong a description. But it is a change worked by the Spirit of God, not by our unaided struggles.

But what is meant by putting to death τὰ μέλη τὰ ἐπὶ τῆς γῆς, 'your limbs which are on the earth'? It seems best (although it is decidedly odd) to treat the phrase as meaning 'your limbs as put to earthly purposes', the use of your limbs (or organs) for sensuality—a meaning which provides a parallel to πορνείαν κ.τ.λ. which follows. In I Cor. vi. 15 St Paul exclaims against making our μέλη the limbs of a harlot by fornication; and in Rom. vii. 4 he speaks of 'being put to death' as regards our former partner (the Law, in that context). It is possible, thus, that 'to put to death the limbs which are on earth' means to be 'dead' as regards their immoral use. Dibelius quotes Reitzenstein to

the effect that in Manichaean writings a parallel can be
found (for what it is worth) to the likening of an abstract
quality to a limb; and in the Hermetic writings (*Corp.
Herm.* XII. 21) ζωὴ καὶ ἀθανασία are μέρη, or, in a variant
reading, μέλη of God (see Dodd, *F.G.*, p. 18).

Theod. Mops. *in loc.* (as also Severianus quoted by Swete
there) says that as the literal body has limbs, so the metaphorical body (i.e. the disposition) has its deeds. But this
does nothing to soften the violence of the metaphor.

Masson suggests taking τὰ μέλη as vocative, representing
an address to Christians as limbs of Christ, making τὰ ἐπὶ
τῆς γῆς (cf. *v.* 2) the object of νεκρώσατε. But it is hard to
believe that, had τὰ μέλη been so intended, it would not
have been explained by a ὑμεῖς or by a τοῦ Χριστοῦ.

Lightfoot virtually takes τὰ μέλη τὰ ἐπὶ τῆς γῆς as = τὸν
παλαιὸν ἄνθρωπον (*v.* 9): 'the old man with all his members
must be pitilessly slain.'

Note that Lightfoot prefers to put a stop after γῆς,
making πορνείαν κ.τ.λ. 'prospective accusatives, which
should be governed directly by some such word as ἀπόθεσθε'
(cf. *v.* 8), though the construction is subsequently broken.
This may well be right, for ἀπόθεσθε is more appropriate
to πορνείαν κ.τ.λ. as νεκρώσατε is to τὰ μέλη.

τὴν πλεονεξίαν ἥτις ἐστὶν εἰδωλολατρία. For this equation, compare Eph. v. 5; and, for the association of
πλεονεξία with sins of sensuality, compare (with M.M.)
Mark vii. 20–23, I Cor. v. 10, vi. 9, 10, II Pet. ii. 14 (cf.
Heb. xiii. 4, 5—the same thought, without the actual word).

If πλεονεξία meant 'acquisitiveness' in any form—simply
the opposite of the desire to *give*—it would be possible to
link it with the fact that the essence of idolatry (whether in a
gross or a refined form) is the desire to *get*, the desire to *use*
God for man's ends, in contrast to true worship, which is
man's desire to yield himself to God's service. But the
evidence points to πλεονεξία meaning 'ruthless and aggres-

sive self-seeking' (see Bauer *s.v.*). If so, the thought is simply the less subtle one that the πλεονέκτης worships Gain as his god (see parallels in Lightfoot from Philo and the Rabbis). I Cor. v. 10, vi. 9, 10 (just adduced) sets idolaters alongside πλεονέκται and ἅρπαγες.

The lists of vices in the N.T., in their different contexts, form some index to the social conditions prevailing in the various places concerned. I Cor. vi. 9–11 reveals the kind of life from which Christianity rescued people. Mark vii. 21, 22 is remarkable, in view of the fact that in *Judaism* the standard of 'morals' (in the ordinarily accepted sense) was generally higher than among the Gentiles.

6. ἡ ὀργὴ τοῦ Θεοῦ. C. H. Dodd in *Romans* (H. and S., 1932), pp. 21 f., points out that Paul rarely uses this phrase. More often, (ἡ) ὀργή stands without the (τοῦ) θεοῦ. Whether or not it is correct to deduce that it is usually viewed as a mere *principle* of retribution, not to be closely associated with the personality of God, it is at any rate clear that the implications of the Gospel do not for one moment leave room for ὀργή as God's *vindictive anger*. Neither μῆνις nor χόλος is used, even in the O.T., of God (see *T.W.N.T.* v, 422). 'Wrath' and 'anger' are therefore unfortunate renderings—for this reason, if not for any reluctance in N.T. usage to couple ὀργή with ὁ θεός: ὀργή may rather be rendered as 'disaster'—the disastrous consequences of sin—and ἡ ὀργὴ τοῦ θεοῦ as 'disaster from God', 'God's terrible judgments'. St Paul only once uses θυμός of God (Rom. ii. 8); but this may be sheer chance: in the LXX, θυμός and ὀργή appear to be virtually synonymous. See note below.

8. ἀπόθεσθε. Does this go with ἐκ τοῦ στόματος, in which case ὀργήν and θυμόν must refer to the *verbal expression* of anger? Or is ἀπόθεσθε a general word, referring to the Christian's divestiture of all the old habits, and is ἐκ τοῦ στόματος then a characterization of αἰσχρολογία—'the foul talk [which issues] from the lips' (cf. Matt. xv. 18)? The latter is redundant, and also rather poor Greek (for τὴν αἰσχρολ. τὴν ἐκ...); and, although it is admittedly a little difficult to restrict the ὀργή and θυμός to *words*, this is perhaps the more likely construction.

τὰ πάντα. Does this refer *back* to all the evils just mentioned (*v.* 5), adding a further characterization of them in terms of other sins, ὀργὴν κ.τ.λ.? More probably it refers *forward*, introducing a new group of sins altogether: 'away with all these, namely...', rather than 'all of these (above mentioned), that is,...'.

ὀργήν, θυμόν. In view of what has been pointed out under *v.* 6 above, it is difficult to press any distinction here (cf. Rev. xvi. 19, xix. 15). But Lightfoot says that Stoic thinkers had distinguished θ. as the outburst of anger from ὀ. as the settled and continuing condition.

κακίαν. This is so general a word that one must allow considerable weight to its context in interpreting it: it seems to range from 'trouble' (with no moral implications), as in 'sufficient unto the day is the κακία thereof', to a definitely culpable attitude of 'wickedness'. Here the latter is obviously required; but it is not so clear whether it can be further defined more precisely as 'malice' (i.e. deliberate intention to do harm). See Lightfoot *in loc.* but also *T.W.N.T. s.v.*

βλασφημίαν. This can, in non-biblical Greek, mean either 'abuse' or, more specifically, 'speech against God'. In biblical uses (see M.M. and *T.W.N.T.*) the latter meaning is uppermost; for even when the object of attack is human, it is usually in some sense representative of the divine, as the Christian community. (Exceptions are Titus iii. 2, II Pet. ii. 10 (?), 11.) Yet, if so, it is difficult to imagine conditions in which any convinced member of the Church would need to be warned against βλασφημία—unless it were under persecution (cf., perhaps, I Cor. xii. 3) or in the company of derisive non-Christians. Perhaps, then, this is a case where it means simply 'detraction', 'slanderous talk' against men.

αἰσχρολογίαν. Simply, 'foul talk'.

9–11. τὸν παλαιὸν ἄνθρωπον...τὸν νέον.... In such a connexion καινός is commoner than νέος, the latter tending to mean 'young' rather than qualitatively 'new'; but here τὸν νέον is followed by a compound of καινός—τὸν ἀνακαινούμενον—and may therefore have been merely chosen for variety, as, perhaps, in Eph. iv. 23f. (where, conversely, the *verb* contains νέος and the *adjective* is καινός). Whether there is a real, and not a merely stylistic, distinction in Matt. ix. 17 βάλλουσιν οἶνον νέον εἰς ἀσκοὺς καινούς is debatable. (I owe much in these observations to Dr J. A. T. Robinson.)

These phrases do not merely mean 'one's old, bad character' and 'the new, Christian character' respectively, as an *individual's* condition: they carry deeper, wider, and more *corporate* associations, inasmuch as they are part of the presentation of the Gospel in terms of the two 'Adams', the two creations. Whereas Adam—Mankind—was created in God's likeness (Gen. i. 26), the Second Adam—new Humanity, Christ—was God's means of re-creating mankind and restoring, renewing (or completing?) that likeness. Whereas Adam was an animate being (a living creature), the Second Adam was an animating spirit (a life-giving Creator) (I Cor. xv. 45). Whereas Adam was 'of the dust of the ground' (Gen. ii. 7), the Second Man is from heaven (I Cor. xv. 47). Thus the terms 'the old humanity', 'the new humanity' derive their force not simply from some individual change of character, but from a corporate re-creation of humanity; and what enables the individual to become transformed from selfishness to a growing effectiveness as a useful member of a group is precisely his 'death' in regard to one type of humanity—the great, collectively

unredeemed Man—and his 'resurrection' into another: we
are back, once more, at the language of baptismal initiation
and incorporation; and we have already seen the relevance
of the metaphor of 'divesting' and 're-clothing' in this
connexion (ii. 15 above).

10. ἀνακαινούμενον. Dr J. A. T. Robinson suggests to
me that the present participle means, not so much that 'the
old Adam' is gradually transformed into something better,
but rather that the new humanity, already existing in
Christ, is progressively actualized in the Christian Church,
until this process culminates in ἐπίγνωσις—full recognition,
both by believers and by the world, of this new humanity
and its implications and demands. (But see next note.)

Conversely, perhaps 'the old Adam' must be regarded as
already dead and done with, and yet as still in process of
being recognized as dead. In II Cor. iv. 16 ὁ ἔξω ἡμῶν
ἄνθρωπος διαφθείρεται...ὁ ἔσω ἡμῶν [ἄνθρωπος] ἀνακαινοῦται
perhaps the same meaning is to be seen: a continual
'mortification' of what is, in fact, already dead, a continual
actualization of an already existing new creation.

εἰς ἐπίγνωσιν κατ' εἰκόνα τοῦ κτίσαντος αὐτόν.

There are several matters for discussion here:

(i) Chrysostom and others took τοῦ κτίσαντος to refer to
Christ; but the allusion to Gen. i. 27 is irresistible: it must
be *God*. αὐτόν = τὸν νέον ἄνθρωπον.

(ii) But in the phrase κατ' εἰκόνα (also from Gen. i. 27),
it may well be that we should see not merely a reference to
the original creation of man 'after God's likeness' (cf.
Eph. iv. 24 κατὰ Θεόν) but, more specifically, to *Christ*,
who is the εἰκών of God (see on i. 15 above). As Adam
was 'made in the likeness of God', so the new Adam,
Christ, '*is*, eternally, God's likeness'. Accordingly, when
God re-creates Man, it is *in the pattern of Christ*, who is God's
Likeness absolutely. See Lightfoot (who, however, rejects
this interpretation) and Masson *in loc.*

(iii) εἰς ἐπίγνωσιν, thus standing absolutely, is difficult. It may mean that the process described *results in knowledge* or *perception*—that response of the whole person to God or Christ which is distinctive of the Christian experience. See A Note on the Knowledge of God, p. 159. Or it may be the recognition of the implications of the ἀνακαινοῦσθαι (see preceding note).

11. The list of social distinctions in this verse throws light on the kind of friction which Christianity had to overcome. Σκύθης appears to represent 'the lowest type of barbarian' (Lightfoot *in loc.*); also no doubt it implied slavery: 'Barbarian slaves were drawn in the main either from Western Asia...or from the tribes round the Black Sea, who were known by the generic name of Scythians. Aristotle defends the enslavement of both classes as natural, on the ground that the Orientals possessed intelligence without courage and the Northerners courage without intelligence'— R. J. G. Mayor in *A Companion to Greek Studies* (Cambridge, 1916), p. 510.

The list is thus logically an overlapping one: Ἕλλην may be the opposite of both Ἰουδαῖος and βάρβαρος; Σκύθης belongs both to the classes βάρβαρος and δοῦλος. It is also (so Lightfoot) particularly appropriate to the Colossian Church. See further, Introduction, pp. 29 f.

πάντα καὶ ἐν πᾶσιν Χριστός. If one pressed the component parts of this phrase, it might mean that Christ *both* is 'everything' (i.e. 'all that matters') and *also* is 'in all' members of the community (or, if it is neuter, 'all things')— i.e. permeating and indwelling all. But perhaps the phrase ought not to be precisely analysed, and is simply a vigorous and emphatic way of saying that Christ is 'absolutely every thing' (or 'all in all' in the general sense which that vague translation of it has come to bear): 'neither race nor class matters: Christ is all that matters.'

Yet, elsewhere in the N.T. where similar expressions

occur, there is no καί: I Cor. xv. 28...ἵνα ᾖ ὁ Θεὸς (τὰ) πάντα ἐν πᾶσιν, Eph. i. 23...τοῦ τὰ πάντα ἐν πᾶσιν πληρουμένου (and cf. the Classical παντάπασιν); and the phrase in I Corinthians, and perhaps also that in Ephesians, is concerned with the relation of God himself to the sum of things —to the cosmos—whereas the Colossians phrase seems to be a term of religious devotion rather than of cosmology or eschatology. Possibly, then, there may be a real difference, and the intrusion of the καί may be a part of the difference and may indicate that, after all, both parts of the phrase must be given recognition. This, indeed, is demanded in Eph. iv. 6 εἷς Θεὸς καὶ Πατὴρ πάντων, ὁ ἐπὶ πάντων καὶ διὰ πάντων καὶ ἐν πᾶσιν.[1] At any rate, our phrase is a very striking one as applied to *Christ*, especially when compared with I Cor. xv. 28 (of *God*). See Introduction, pp. 3 ff., and note on i. 15–23 above.

12. **ὡς ἐκλεκτοὶ τοῦ Θεοῦ ἅγιοι καὶ ἠγαπημένοι.** All the three 'terms' (chosen, holy, beloved) 'are transferred from the Old Covenant to the New, from Israel after the flesh to Israel after the Spirit'—Lightfoot.

ἐκλεκτός is not found elsewhere in the Pauline epistles (outside the Pastorals) except in Rom. viii. 33, xvi. 13; but ἐκλογή occurs in Rom. ix. 11, xi. 5, 7, 28, and I Thess. i. 4, as well as in non-Pauline writings; and ἐκλέγεσθαι is strikingly used in I Cor. i. 27, 28; also καλεῖν, κλῆσις, κλητός, several times. Side by side with this conception of God's *choice* and *summons* comes that of God's *love*: in Rom. ix. 13 the ἐκλογή passage reaches its climax in τὸν Ἰακὼβ ἠγάπησα, τὸν δὲ Ἡσαῦ ἐμίσησα; in xi. 28 the Jews are κατὰ...τὴν ἐκλογὴν ἀγαπητοί; and in I Thess. i. 4 the ἐκλογή of Christians is associated with their being ἀδελφοὶ ἠγαπημένοι ὑπὸ τοῦ Θεοῦ.

Thus the Church is the true Israel, owing its call to God's

---

[1] M. S. Enslin, *The Ethics of Paul* (New York, 1930), p. 35, n. 62, cites Macrobius, *Sat.* i. 20. 11, where Heracles is τὸν ἐν πᾶσι καὶ διὰ πάντων ἥλιον.

service entirely to his initiative and unmerited love; and
Christians may so be appealed to to 'clothe themselves'
with a corresponding character: they not only have Christ's
example (ὁ Κύριος in *v.* 13 is probably rightly interpreted by
the variant reading ὁ Χριστός), but they have the new
character, given to them as God's free gift, an endowment
put on like a garment.

What St Paul chooses for mention here might be called
the 'ordinary' virtues—precisely those which reduce or
eliminate friction: ready sympathy, a generous spirit, a
humble disposition, willingness to make concessions,
patience, forbearance.

14. 'And on top of all the other "articles of clothing"—
in addition to the rest—put on ἀγάπη, which holds them
together and completes them' (or, reading the variant
ἑνότητος, D* G Ambst, 'unifies them').

This paraphrase assumes:

(i) That ἐπὶ πᾶσιν τούτοις means 'in addition to these',
though it may possibly be elative, 'above all'.

(ii) That σύνδεσμος here has some more general meaning
than in ii. 19 above (see note there).

(iii) That τῆς τελειότητος (or the variant reading ἑνότητος)
is a descriptive genitive (but in Eph. iv. 3 ἐν τῷ σ. τῆς
εἰρήνης the genitive is more probably a defining one—'the
bond which is peace').

(iv) That it is the virtues which are thus bound together,
though Masson inclines to think that it is the persons concerned: cf. ii. 2 συμβιβασθέντες ἐν ἀγάπῃ.

Commentators, at least from Wettstein onwards, quote
Simplicius' saying (in *Epictet.* p. 208) that the Pythagoreans
honoured φιλία more than any other virtue and called it
σύνδεσμον...πασῶν τῶν ἀρετῶν. See also Plato *Polit.* 310 A
(for σύνδεσμος ἀρετῆς in a different sense), and a number of
other references for σύνδεσμος in H. Chadwick, 'All things to
all men' (*J.N.T.S.* I, no. 4 (May 1955), p. 273). If there were

evidence that σύνδεσμος was an article of attire, the phrase
would be still easier to grasp; but 'belt' or 'girdle' is not
attested among its meanings. For an ill sense (? = 'fetter'
or 'chain'), see Acts viii. 23 (alluding to Isa. lviii. 6, 9—so
also Barnabas iii. 3 and 5). Ignatius, *Trall*. iii. 1, uses it as
'college' (of apostles).

The λόγος (as Lightfoot on i. 17 shows) was spoken of by
Philo as the δεσμός of everything. Is it possible that St Paul
—and, for that matter, the Pythagoreans just quoted—were
suggesting that the physical and moral realms both show a
principle of coherence? For the Christian, Christ is that
principle in both realms: in him the universe coheres (i. 17),
and it is ἀγάπη (which Christ embodies) which gives
coherence to conduct. This thought could be in keeping
with the way in which in i. 15 ff. Christ is related first to the
universe and then also to the salvation of men.

In Rom. xiii. 10 ἀγάπη is spoken of, with similar inclusiveness, as πλήρωμα νόμου.

15. ἡ εἰρήνη τοῦ Χριστοῦ βραβευέτω.... βραβευέτω is
apparently one of St Paul's athletic metaphors (see on ii. 18
above).

'The peace of Christ' seems to mean the peace which
Christ brings (cf. John xiv. 27), that is the peace which is
the result of obedience to him: obedience to the will of
Christ is to be the 'umpire' in their hearts, settling conflicts
of will and bringing co-ordination and direction to life.

It is to such peace, the apostle says, that they were sum-
moned,—ἐν ἑνὶ σώματι, as members of a single body; i.e.
(perhaps) because, as Christians, they were already members of that one body. It would be possible to treat the
phrase as a final or a consecutive clause—'so that you may
be', or 'so as to become'; but the other interpretation is in
keeping with the fact that the Christians' status is already
achieved. By surrendering his body to death (i. 22), Christ
has made Christians members of his risen Body.

16. ὁ λόγος τοῦ Χριστοῦ: i.e. the Gospel, the 'Word' uttered by Christ in his life and ministry and through his person, and repeated by each Christian as he proclaims the Gospel by life and witness.

ἐνοικείτω κ.τ.λ. Problems of punctuation and interpretation arise:

(i) Does ἐν πάσῃ σοφίᾳ go with ἐνοικείτω or with διδάσκοντες?

(ii) Does ψαλμοῖς κ.τ.λ. go primarily with διδάσκοντες καὶ νουθετοῦντες ἑαυτούς or with ᾄδοντες?

It would be possible to translate: 'let "the word of Christ" make its home among (or perhaps within) you in all its richness, in the form of every kind of wisdom, while you teach and admonish one another with psalms, hymns, and spiritual songs, singing...'; or '...in all its richness, while you teach and admonish one another in all wisdom, singing in psalms etc....'

On the face of it, it is not obvious how one instructs and admonishes with psalms etc.; but there is no denying that Eph. v. 19 leaves no choice but to '*speak* to one another in psalms' etc.; and presumably the use of music and utterances of praise may be didactic (cf. I Cor. xiv. 26 ff.).

ἐν πάσῃ σοφίᾳ does not offer a sure clue to our choice either, since in i. 9 it seems to be more or less descriptive of τὴν ἐπίγνωσιν τοῦ θελήματος αὐτοῦ (see notes there), as it might be here of the contents of the 'word', whereas in iv. 5 it is as clearly descriptive of the Christians' way of doing things, and might thus qualify 'teach and admonish'.

The choice seems evenly balanced, unless Ephesians is to be accepted as a reliable pointer to the meaning here.

For the indwelling 'word', Lohmeyer compares Ps. xxxvii (LXX xxxvi). 31, of the indwelling Law of God.

διδάσκοντες καὶ νουθετοῦντες.... Grammatically an anacoluthon, but easily understandable.

ἐν τῇ χάριτι. Whether the meaning is 'gratefully' or 'by

NOTES [iii. 16, 17; iii. 18–iv. 1

the grace (of God)' or 'in the (realm of God's) grace' is uncertain. The presence or absence of the definite article (about which the MSS. are divided) does not necessarily determine the answer. The context favours 'gratefully' (so Dibelius and Bauer *s.v.*); Lightfoot is strongly in favour of referring it (especially if τῇ be read) to God's grace, and Lohmeyer also favours this. Again, it is doubtful whether to attach the phrase to what precedes or to what follows. On the whole the easiest sense, at any rate, is 'gratefully singing...'.

The MS. evidence is:

ἐν τῇ χάριτι p⁴⁶ ℵ BD* G 1739 *al* Cl;

ἐν χάριτι ℵ*A *pm* ϛ;

omit Cᶜ 1 *pc.*

It looks as though τῇ were the true reading, and subsequent scribes had encountered as much difficulty in interpreting it as we do.

ἐν ταῖς καρδίαις. The vocal praise is to be accompanied by an inward *spirit* of praise. Cf., in a slightly different connexion, I Cor. xiv. 15.

17. Cf. I Cor. x. 31.

τῷ Θεῷ Πατρί. DGI *pl* Cl ϛ read τῷ Θεῷ καὶ Πατρί. See on i. 3.

iii. 18–iv. 1. *Life within a household, as it is affected by Christianity.*

If Colossians is earlier than Ephesians and I Peter, here is the earliest of all surviving examples of this sort of admonition in its Christian form. There are scattered injunctions in earlier epistles (e.g. I Cor. vii, regarding slaves, husbands, and wives); but they are directed to specific problems rather than, as here, to the relationships of the ordinary life of each day.

Here, then, for the first time we meet in writing a compact little section of Christian instruction such as was probably being regularly given orally by responsible leaders in the various Christian communities. Other examples soon follow: Eph. v. 22–vi. 9, I Pet. ii. 13 ff., Titus ii. 1–10, I Tim. ii. 8 ff., vi. 1 ff., *Didache* iv. 9–11, Barnabas xix. 5 and 7, I Clem. i. 3, xxi. 6–9, Polycarp, *Phil.* iv, v.

Pagan prototypes were, however, already current; for although the examples cited by Dibelius *in loc.* are in part later (Epictetus, Diogenes Laertius, Pseudo-Phocylides), there are also, as he points out, instances of household relationships being mentioned in panegyrics of an earlier period (e.g. Polybius, *Hist.* XVIII. 41. 8, 9, of Attalus), and, indeed, it is a subject which moralists must inevitably have discussed. In Judaism, Philo, *de Decalogo* 165–7 contains comparable matter, and so does Josephus, *contra Apionem* II. 199–210 (but it is doubtful whether this is earlier than, at best, the very latest parts of the N.T.). Ecclus. xxx. 1–13 (how to treat your son) and xlii. 5, 9–11 (about correcting your children, and keeping strict watch over your daughter) make strange reading, side by side with the New Testament.

We have, thus, material for a comparative study of household instructions in paganism, Judaism, and the Christian communities. What is claimed as the outstanding Christian innovation, as contrasted with the pagan examples, is the stress upon the reciprocal nature of the duties. Anticipations of this in pagan thought, if not much in pagan practice, can, no doubt, be cited (e.g. Euripides, *Ion*, 854 ff.; and see Max Pohlenz, *Die Stoa* (Göttingen, 1948), pp. 135 f. for Stoic thought on the matter); but the stress lies elsewhere. Even Judaism, it has been said, like all the ancient religions, had assumed that all the rights were on one side and the duties on the other. But here it is made evident that with God 'the claims of the slave are as real as the claims of the master' (Lightfoot on iii. 25). All said and done, however, the greatest distinctiveness of the

Christian ethical teaching lies not in its contents so much as in its motives, its quality, and its conditions: ἐν Χριστῷ is *the* new factor.[1]

The note of *submission*—ὑποταγή, ὑποτάσσεσθαι (cf. I Cor. xi. 3 ff., xiv. 34)—is, none the less, a clear one, and one which perplexes the modern Christian reader—unless, indeed, a clear distinction is intended between submission and *inferiority*. Yet, whatever advance may have been made since New Testament times, under the guidance of the Holy Spirit, towards a deeper understanding of personal relations, the really remarkable thing is, not that the N.T. writers regarded women as essentially subordinate—this was a legacy from Judaism itself, let alone any pagan influences, which could not rapidly be lost—nor that slavery was accepted as inevitable for the time being, but rather that household life was so transformed 'in the Lord' that each person was seen as precious to God, and that husbands and masters recognized that they had duties no less than rights. Cf. I Cor. vii. 4, I Pet. iii. 7.

Comparing the N.T. passages on these matters with one another, Colossians gives special prominence to the slavery question (no doubt because of Onesimus, as commentators observe); but Ephesians is more developed than Colossians in its extended analogy between the 'marriage' of Christ and his Church and the husband-wife relationship, and in its appeal to the Decalogue in connexion with filial obedience. I Peter is notable for its appeal to the example of Christ in its exhortation to slaves (household servants, οἰκέται); and it closely couples the injunctions to civic obedience

[1] It is interesting that 'while Paul uses the formula "in Christ" of the mutual duties of husband and wife, parent and child, he does not use it of the mutual duties of masters and servants'—Best, *One Body*, p. 27, n. 1. Best suggests that this is because the master-servant relationship did not itself (as the family relationship did) form a natural unity. Even if a husband or wife was not a Christian, there was some natural bond, so that if one partner was ἐν Χριστῷ the other might be considered so also (I Cor. vii. 12–16); but not so with slave and master.

with the household section (whereas this is not the case in Rom. xiii). There are striking features in the corresponding injunctions in the Apostolic Fathers, but these must not be pursued here. For a later Christian example, see T. R. Glover, *The Conflict of Religions in the Early Roman Empire* (Methuen, 1909), pp. 264ff. (on Clement of Alexandria).

For some discussion of slavery, see the notes on Philemon and Introduction, p. 10. In general, see the valuable tables and discussion in Selwyn, *I Peter*.

18. ἀνῆκεν. This word, although without the Stoic associations of τὸ καθῆκον, would, in itself, fit easily enough into pagan ethical teaching. But if so, the following ἐν Κυρίῳ is the more pointed: it is incorporation in the Christian community which makes a new thing of conduct. In Philem. 8, τὸ ἀνῆκον = 'that which is the right thing to do'. The imperfect tense may be regarded as an idiom comparable to ἔδει, ἐδύνατο etc. (so D.-B., § 358; though see Lightfoot *in loc.*).

19. μὴ πικραίνεσθε and (*v.* 21) **μὴ ἐρεθίζετε** speak of friction caused by impatience and thoughtless 'nagging', and remind us that the new life in Christ transforms relationship on the 'ordinary' levels, as well as conquering the spectacular vices. In Eph. vi. 4 the parallel to μὴ ἐρεθίζετε is μὴ παροργίζετε. The sensitive understanding of children, with the realization that they might become discouraged and lose heart (ἵνα μὴ ἀθυμῶσιν), is a striking feature of this new chapter in social history. It would be unjust to paganism, to be sure, to describe it only in lurid terms of infanticide and broken homes. J. W. Mackail's *Select Epigrams from the Greek Anthology* (London, 1906), pp. 42f., points out some beautiful features of the home life of the world reflected in that Anthology. And Judaism, even more obviously, was able to show splendid examples of such happiness. But the fact remains that the relationship ἐν Κυρίῳ was new, and derived its impetus from Christ himself.

20. εὐάρεστόν ἐστιν ἐν Κυρίῳ. Lightfoot takes εὐάρεστον in a secular sense, 'commendable', and renders ἐν Κυρίῳ 'as judged by a Christian standard'. But elsewhere in the Bible, with few exceptions, εὐάρεστος appears to mean pleasing *to God* (contrast ἀνθρωπάρεσκοι, *v.* 22). If so, then ἐν Κυρίῳ must either represent a sort of conditional clause—'provided that the children's obedience is ἐν Κυρίῳ, on a truly Christian level of motive'—or must be reckoned an unnecessary addition; or else must be taken as an odd expression for 'to the Lord', as though it were a plain dative after εὐάρεστον. Against the last suggestion is the fact that in the LXX εὐάρεστος does not occur with such a construction, and εὐαρεστεῖν, when used with ἐν (only once, and then only according to one MS.) or with ἐναντίον, does not correspond to a Hebrew verb of *pleasing* at all, but usually to a verb of *conduct* (to 'walk' before God). Possibly the 'conditional' interpretation is best: cf. I Cor. vii. 39 μόνον ἐν Κυρίῳ, Phil. ii. 19 ἐλπίζω δὲ ἐν Κυρίῳ Ἰησοῦ....

22. ὀφθαλμοδουλίαις (or -ίᾳ) is not found before the Pauline writings (here and Eph. vi. 6), and may be of the apostle's own coining. It might mean 'merely such service as can be seen', i.e. superficial work—not dusting behind the ornaments, not sweeping under the wardrobe. But both in Colossians and Ephesians the context suggests rather going through the outward movements of the work *without a corresponding keenness of will behind them* (so Masson): μὴ... ὡς ἀνθρωπάρεσκοι, ἀλλ' ἐν ἁπλότητι καρδίας (lit. 'in singleness of heart', i.e. 'in honesty', 'with no ulterior motives', cf. I Chron. xxix. 17, where ἐν ἁπλ. κ.=בְּיֹשֶׁר לְבָבִי, 'in the uprightness of my heart'); so *v.* 23 ἐκ ψυχῆς (for which cf. I Pet. i. 22 ἐκ καρδίας). See *E. T.* LIX, no. 9 (June 1948), p. 250.

24. τὴν ἀνταπόδοσιν τῆς κληρονομίας: 'the reward, namely, to enter the promised land' (see on i. 12 above). This, in view of ἀνταπόδοσις and the O.T. use of the 'inheritance' idea, seems a probable interpretation. On the other hand, κληρονομία can mean simply 'inherited property'; and the strange ἀπὸ Κυρίου (without the definite article) suggests to some that the metaphor is of a slave paradoxically receiving property—as though he were the son, the κληρονόμος (cf. Gal. iv. 1–7)—from 'one who is his Master'. See Lightfoot *in loc.*

The answer to the suggestion that the N.T. sometimes speaks in apparently mercenary terms of reward and punishment is that the 'reward' is always something to do with our relations with God, and the 'punishment' is deprivation of his fellowship. The κληρονομία, the dwelling in the 'promised land' or the possession of the Kingdom of God, is precisely that life in the presence of God which mercenary-mindedness would make impossible. So, when St Paul says (*v.* 25) that 'the dishonest person shall receive the dishonesty that he has committed', the meaning is that dishonesty brings its own nemesis—exclusion from a position which is possible only for one who is honest with God.

τῷ Κυρίῳ Χριστῷ.... Only here and in Rom. xvi. 18 does St Paul speak of 'the Lord Christ' (or 'our Lord Christ' in Romans); and in both places (it is contended) he is contrasting Christ *as Lord* with other lords. (In this context it is the slave's master who provides the implied contrast: 'it is *Christ* who must be *your* Master'.) Whether 'Christ' is here merely a proper name (a mere alternative for 'Jesus'), or something more, is another matter. It may still carry here at least a trace of its use as a title. But it is true (see on ii. 6 above) that, in the Pauline writings generally, 'Christ' has all but become a name rather than a title. See N. A. Dahl, 'Die Messianität Jesu bei Paulus' in *Studia Paulina*, p. 84, and V. Taylor, *Names, s.v.*

δουλεύετε. Is this indicative or imperative? Imperative (*pace* Lightfoot), to judge by the following γάρ (which loses point if it is an indicative); and no doubt in *v.* 23 ἐργάζεσθε is imperative.

25. προσωπολημψία. An interesting word, in that it seems not to appear before the N.T., and to have been coined in Christian circles, though from O.T. metal. The Hebrew idiom for 'to show partiality' is 'to accept the face' (נשא פנים); this is occasionally represented in the LXX by πρόσωπον λαμβάνειν (e.g. Lev. xix. 15, Job xlii. 8, Mal. ii. 9, Ecclus. iv. 22, 27; but often another verb is used such as θαυμάζω); and it is from this that the Christian writers evidently formed this abstract noun (Rom. ii. 11, Eph. vi. 9, Col. iii. 25, Jas. ii. 1), a personal noun προσωπολήμπτης (Acts x. 34), a verb προσωπολημπτέω (Jas. ii. 9), and a portentous negative adverb ἀπροσωπολήμπτως (I Pet. i. 17). Gal. ii. 6 has πρόσωπον...οὐ λαμβάνει, just like the LXX.

iv. 1. ἰσότητα. In the context, evidently 'fairness', 'equity', not 'equality' of status.

iv. 2–6. *Various admonitions.*

2. γρηγοροῦντες is no doubt primarily metaphorical— 'being vigilant' in maintaining prayer, or, more probably, 'being vigilant', as opposed to lethargic, while at prayer. But possibly it contains also a vivid flash of reminiscence of the literal sleep which St Paul had heard about in the story of the Passion (Matt. xxvi. 40, 41, etc.), or of the Transfiguration (Luke ix. 32). Cf. on *v.* 12 below.

ἐν εὐχαριστίᾳ. Cf. Phil. iv. 6.

3. θύραν. For this metaphor, cf. I Cor. xvi. 9, II Cor. ii. 12. It seems to mean 'an opportunity to preach the Gospel'—an 'opening', as we say. But in Acts xiv. 27, ἤνοιξεν τοῖς ἔθνεσιν θύραν πίστεως possibly means 'he has given to the Gentiles a means of access, namely faith'. And in Rev. iii. 8 does it signify free access into the Kingdom of God? Cf. the words of the *Te Deum*, *aperuisti credentibus regna caelorum.*

τὸ μυστήριον τοῦ Χριστοῦ. See on i. 26, 27 above. It is a particularly pointed paradox to speak of τὸ μυστήριον in connexion with φανεροῦν (v. 4), when that verb means (as it does here) a public manifestation. But in itself the verb is suitable enough (as Masson says) for the communication of a revelation privately.

4. ὡς δεῖ με λαλῆσαι. The natural interpretation is either 'in the way in which it is right that I should speak it' (the rightness being viewed in reference to any given circumstances in which the apostle is called upon to speak), or 'since I am bound (by my vocation as an evangelist, or by the necessity of evangelism in God's plan for the world, cf. Mark xiii. 10, Acts xxiii. 11) to speak it'. The latter keeps strictly to the meaning of δεῖ, 'it is necessary'. Yet a thing which is *necessary* if one is to do right in certain conditions is virtually what one *ought* to do (see examples in *T.W.N.T.* II, 21 f. from both secular and biblical Greek). It would seem, therefore, reasonable to translate (with A.V. and R.V.) 'as I ought to speak'; cf. πῶς δεῖ, v. 6 below. To construe the phrase as denoting the contents of the φανέρωσις ('until I can make clear to the authorities why I cannot help telling it'—E. J. Goodspeed in his translation, 1923) is unnatural, and drives a gratuitous wedge between this passage and the Ephesians parallel (vi. 20), where such an interpretation is impossible.

5. Ἐν σοφίᾳ κ.τ.λ. I.e. 'Behave with tact towards non-Christians'; cf. I Thess. iv. 12. St Paul probably has in mind the difference between bold, uncompromising witness to the Christian allegiance when occasion offers, and a harsh, unloving, tactless obtruding of it at the wrong time.

τὸν καιρὸν ἐξαγοραζόμενοι. The same sort of phrase appears in Dan. ii. 8 (וּבְנִין) rendered in both the LXX and Theodotion's version as καιρὸν ὑμεῖς ἐξαγοράζετε; but there it means 'gain time', 'temporize', and thus seems to throw no light on its meaning here.

Commentators, ancient and modern, have wrestled with it, both here and in Eph. v. 16 (where it is the same except for the order of the words). What is the metaphor? Is it from the market in general, or from the slave-market in particular? Does it mean 'buy up the entire stock of opportunity'—eagerly seize every opportunity; or does it mean 'buy out of slavery—emancipate—the opportunity' from the control of Evil into whose hands it has fallen?

Robinson, *Eph. in loc.*, points out that the former sense (that of 'making a corner' in the market, 'buying up the whole stock') would be properly expressed by συναγοράζειν or συνωνεῖσθαι, and that no instance of the verb compounded with ἐξ- provides a convincing parallel for this sense. He therefore adopts the second (the 'rescue' or 'emancipation' metaphor), which has support from (among others) Oecumenius (cited by Abbott on Eph. v. 16), Theod. Mops., and Severianus (in J. A. Cramer's *Catenae Graecorum Patrum in N.T.* (Oxford, 1842–4)).

It seems, however, slightly bizarre to treat ὁ καιρός as a person needing help (though it appears that some scribe regarded it as capable of personification when he wrote, in Rom. xii. 11, τῷ καιρῷ (instead of τῷ Κυρίῳ) δουλεύοντες—unless this is a pure slip of the pen); and it is perhaps more natural, after all, to treat it as a commodity to be eagerly bought (ἐξ- 'intensive', as Abbott *loc. cit.* takes it).

This sense fits the Ephesians context (ὅτι αἱ ἡμέραι πονηραί εἰσιν) quite as well as the other sense; and it is perhaps relevant to recall the parables of the hidden treasure and the supremely valuable pearl (Matt. xiii).

καιρός is an important word in N.T. thought. Admittedly, it often seems to mean no more than a *point* of time in contrast to χρόνος, which is usually of *duration*; and it is sometimes used side by side with χρόνος; see Acts i. 6, 7, I Thess. v. 1 (the two together). Yet καιρός is also used as 'time for some given action', 'significant time', 'God's time', 'opportunity', in contrast to χρόνος or ὥρα when

they mean mere passive 'lapse of time', or time measured by
the calendar or the clock (although, again, there are
exceptions, when χρόνος seems to mean *significant* time: Acts
i. 6, as above, vii. 17, Gal. iv. 4, I Pet. i. 20, or when ὥρα
means the *crucial* moment: Matt. xxvi. 45, Mark xiv. 35, 41,
Luke xxii. 53, John ii. 4, vii. 30, viii. 20, xii. 23, xvi. 27, xix.
27). See Cullmann, *C.T.*, ch. 1, J. A. T. Robinson, *In the
End, God*... (James Clarke, 1950), ch. IV.

6. ἐν χάριτι perhaps means 'gracious', 'charming'—a
use of χάρις which reminds one of its inseparable link
with the more Hellenistic and aesthetic side of its meaning, and which does linger in parts of the N.T. See
J. Moffatt, *Grace in the New Testament* (London, 1931),
pp. 293 f.

ἅλατι ἠρτυμένος perhaps means 'wholesome' (cf. Eph.
iv. 29); but it may well mean 'witty', 'not insipid', for
Classical literature provides familiar parallels for 'salt' in
such a connexion: see Moffatt, just cited. (Note, however, that Plutarch *de Garrul.* 23, p. 514f, which is sometimes quoted, is not really apposite; it is about seasoning *life*
with *words* as one seasons food with salt; it says nothing
about seasoning *words* with *wit*: χάριν τινὰ παρασκευάζοντες
ἀλλήλοις, ὥσπερ ἁλσὶ τοῖς λόγοις ἐφηδύνουσι τὴν διατριβὴν
καὶ τὴν πρᾶξιν..., '...they seek to ingratiate themselves
with each other by seasoning with the salt of conversa-
tion the pastime or business in which they happen to
be engaged'—W. C. Hembold's translation in the Loeb
edition.)

If so, this verse is a plea to Christians not to confuse loyal
godliness with a dull, graceless insipidity. If a Christian is
ever difficult company, it ought to be because he demands
too much, not too little, from his fellows' responsiveness and
wit. As in the preceding paragraph (see on iii. 19, 21),
the importance of the small things of life here becomes
noticeable.

iv. 7–9. *Personal news will be conveyed by Tychicus and Onesimus.*

This paragraph is a reminder of how much was done by word of mouth. A letter was a comparatively rare vehicle, and its contents and purpose would be correspondingly specialized: the ordinary remarks would be transmitted verbally, especially when there were urgent doctrinal and pastoral matters demanding such writing-space as there was. For the persons and circumstances, see Introduction, pp. 25 ff. Eph. vi. 21 f. is in part identical with this paragraph.

7. **διάκονος.** There is nothing in the context to suggest that this is used here in a technical sense, as 'Deacon'. It probably means 'servant of the Lord', 'minister in Christian work', in a general sense. Cf. on i. 23 above.

σύνδουλος, that is, a fellow-slave, with Paul, of Jesus Christ.

ἐν Κυρίῳ. See on i. 2, iii. 18–iv. 1, iii. 20 above.

8. **ἔπεμψα.** Like ἀνέπεμψα in Philem. 12, demonstrably an 'epistolary aorist', to be rendered by an English present tense, for Tychicus is going with this letter (*v.* 7).

iv. 10–17. *Messages and injunctions.*

For the persons and circumstances, again see Introduction, pp. 25 ff.

10. **ὁ συναιχμάλωτός μου.** It is true that in Acts xxvii. 2 Aristarchus is a companion of the prisoner St Paul on his voyage to Rome; and it is sometimes alleged that St Paul would, in such conditions, not have been allowed a companion unless that companion had also himself been a prisoner. But there are reasons for taking the word metaphorically, as meaning a prisoner *of Christ*, as St Paul also was:

(i) αἰχμάλωτος is properly 'a prisoner *of war*', which St Paul, literally speaking, was not. 'Fellow-prisoners', in a general sense, is expressed by συνδεδεμένοι, Heb. xiii. 3, or by some other use of δέω, etc. (cf. δέσμιος in Philem. 1).

(ii) συναιχμάλωτος occurs also in Rom. xvi. 7, of Andronicus and Junias, and in Philem. 23, where, as Lightfoot remarks, 'this honourable title is withheld from Aristarchus and given to Epaphras'. It is hard to believe that both Aristarchus and Epaphras were, or had been, literally fellow-prisoners with St Paul, not to mention Andronicus and Junias.

It seems best, therefore, to see in the word the same metaphor—*Christus Victor*—as in II Cor. ii. 14, '...God, which always leadeth us in triumph in Christ' (R.V.). Cf. σύνδουλος (of Epaphras again, in i. 7 above). But if Christians are taken prisoner by Christ, they, in their turn, have to assume the offensive against his enemies: II Cor. x. 5 αἰχμαλωτίζοντες πᾶν νόημα εἰς τὴν ὑπακοὴν τοῦ Χριστοῦ. Cf. συνστρατιώτης in Philem. 2. See G. Kittel in *T.W.N.T.* s.v. αἰχμάλωτος.

περὶ οὗ ἐλάβετε ἐντολάς, κ.τ.λ. There is no telling when or how these instructions had been conveyed. Had there been a previous letter from St Paul?

11. οἱ ὄντες κ.τ.λ. It is not quite clear (nor very important) how to punctuate:

(i) ...ὁ λεγόμενος Ἰοῦστος. οἱ ὄντες..., οὗτοι μόνοι..., i.e. 'As for the Jews, only these...';

(ii) ...ὁ λεγόμενος Ἰοῦστος, οἱ ὄντες ἐκ περιτομῆς. οὗτοι μόνοι..., i.e. '...who are Jews. These are the only ones...'; or, possibly,

(iii) accent οἵ, ὄντες..., and construe '...who, being Jews, are the only ones...', οὗτοι then being redundant but intelligible.

In any case, this group, as Jewish Christians friendly with the apostle, are distinguished from the names which follow; and this is the chief evidence that St Luke (*v.* 14) was a Gentile.

Note that the two Evangelists, Luke and Mark (if indeed this is the Evangelist), are together here with St Paul.

τὴν βασιλείαν τοῦ Θεοῦ. See note on i. 13, 14 (note (v)) above.

12. ἀγωνιζόμενος. It is just possible (cf. Lightfoot *in loc.*) that this is a reminiscence of the Lucan version of Christ's 'agony' (that is, 'struggle', 'contest') of prayer in the Garden (Luke xxii. 44). Cf. on iv. 2 above.

πεπληροφορημένοι. Does this mean 'complete' ('filled'), or 'convinced'? The verb clearly means 'convince' in Rom. iv. 21, xiv. 5; and 'complete' (or 'fulfil') in II Tim. iv. 5, 17. In Luke i. 1 also, 'completed' (or 'fulfilled') seems the only suitable sense; there is no evidence in the N.T. or outside it for the A.V. translation 'most surely believed'. (In the present verse, the A.V. has 'complete'.)

Decision depends in part on how—

ἐν παντὶ θελήματι τοῦ Θεοῦ is interpreted. Conceivably it might be construed with ἵνα σταθῆτε (so Delling in *T.W.N.T. s. v. πλήρης*, etc.): 'that you may stand firm in all the will of God, mature and complete (or convinced)'. Or it might indicate that with which they were 'filled' (though this does not yield very good sense). More probably it describes the circumstances of the verbs: 'that you may stand firm, mature and convinced, engaged in doing all the will of God'. 'Convinced' thus seems the best sense for πεπληροφορημένοι here.

15. τὴν...ἐκκλησίαν. See A Note on Christian Greetings in Letters, p. 153.

16. τὴν ἐκ Λαοδικίας. Theod. Mops. and Theodoret held this to mean a letter written by the Laodicean Christians to Paul, possibly accusing the Colossians, which Paul now wishes them to hear. It is much more likely that it was a Pauline letter to Laodicea which the Colossians are now to receive in exchange for the letter addressed to them. Already by Theodore's time there was a forged 'Letter to

the Laodiceans' to supply the lack of anything in the Pauline letters representing it (see H. B. Swete, *Theodore*, p. 310). But why, then, does Paul address messages to *Laodicean* Christians in this letter to Colossae? See Introduction, p. 18.

iv. 18. *Autograph farewell.*

18. Very moving in its brevity and pathos. But note (with Lightfoot) that the reference to 'bonds' is not chiefly a matter of pathos but of authority; cf. Philem. 9.

For St Paul's own hand, see I Cor. xvi. 21, Gal. vi. 11, II Thess. iii. 17 (cf. ii. 2), Philem. 19.

For the greetings and farewell formulae, see A Note on Christian Greetings in Letters, p. 153.

THE EPISTLE TO PHILEMON

1–3. *Greeting.*

For the forms of greeting and farewell, see A Note on Christian Greetings in Letters, p. 153.

For the circumstances and persons, see Introduction, pp. 14 ff.

1. δέσμιος. It was a proud claim to be in prison for the sake of the Gospel, and Theod. Mops. *in loc.* notes the skilful diplomacy with which St Paul uses this term to enforce his appeal for what must seem a trifling sacrifice in comparison with imprisonment. Cf. *v.* 9 below, and Eph. iii. 1, iv. 1, II Tim. i. 8. On the *metaphorical* idea of being 'a prisoner of Christ', see on συναιχμάλωτος, Col. iv. 10.

συνεργῷ. The word is applied to several different persons in the N.T.: see *v.* 24 below, and Rom. xvi. 3, 9, 21, II Cor. viii. 23, Phil. ii. 25, iv. 3, Col. iv. 11, I Thess. iii. 2 (some MSS.)—not to mention less specific uses.

2. τῇ ἀδελφῇ. See on *v.* 16 below.

συνστρατιώτῃ. Elsewhere in the N.T. only in Phil. ii. 25, of Epaphroditus. It seems to be a metaphor—'fellow-campaigner'. See, again, on Col. iv. 10 (συναιχμάλωτος).

4–7. *Thanksgiving.*

4. πάντοτε. With εὐχαριστῶ, i.e. 'I thank God every time your name comes to my lips'; see on Col. i. 3.

μνείαν σου ποιούμενος. The phrase is used also in Rom. i. 9, Eph. i. 16, I Thess. i. 2. It is a question whether it means to remind *oneself* or *another*—'remember' or 'mention' (cf. the two senses of μνημονεύειν, as in Heb. xi. 15, 22). Lightfoot on I Thess. i. 2 (in *Notes on Epistles of St Paul*, Macmillan, 1895) adduces Plato, *Protag.* 317e, *Phaedr.* 254a for 'mention'; and M.M. *s.v.* quote at least one example

from a papyrus (second century A.D.) where it clearly means
'mention' in prayer to the gods (other examples are less
clear); and (as Lightfoot points out) there is an unambiguous phrase for 'remember', namely μνείαν ἔχειν,
II Tim. i. 3. The balance of probability seems thus to
favour 'mention'. On μνεία in Phil. i. 3, however, see
Schubert, 'Form and Function' (as on Col. i. 3).

5. τὴν ἀγάπην καὶ τὴν πίστιν κ.τ.λ. This apparently
simple expression presents difficulties when it is analysed:
are both the ἀγάπη and the πίστις directed towards both
the Lord Jesus and also towards all God's people (οἱ ἅγιοι)?
If so, what does πίστις mean? Presumably, 'faithfulness',
'reliability'; cf. III John 5 πιστὸν ποιεῖς ὃ ἐὰν ἐργάσῃ εἰς
τοὺς ἀδελφούς ('. . .it is loyal of you to do anything you can
for the brothers'—E. J. Goodspeed's translation, 1923). Or,
alternatively, is the ἀγάπη directed towards God's people,
and the πίστις towards the Lord? If so, the structure of the
sentence is strikingly 'chiastic' (i.e. *chi*-shaped, of the form
a b b a—(a) ἀγάπη (b) πίστις (b) Κύριος (a) ἅγιοι). H. W.
Moule (in his interleaved Greek Testament) compares
Ps. cxiii. 5 f. for the grouping together, first of two qualities,
and then of two spheres in which they respectively operate
(although there the order is *a b a b*, not chiastic). He also
notes, on Col. i. 4, that that verse is comparable to the
present verse in Philem. There seems to be no objection,
then, to accepting the latter interpretation (chiasmus is
common enough in St Paul); and, in that case, it is possible,
though not inevitable, to take πίστις in the characteristically
Pauline sense, of 'trust' in the Lord Jesus. Eph. i. 15
contains an unambiguous sentence in which the parts are
thus distributed; and see next note.

πρὸς τὸν Κύριον. There is a *v.l.* εἰς (but no *v.l.* πρός to
the εἰς before πάντας τοὺς ἁγίους). πρός is paralleled by
I Thess. i. 8 (ἡ πίστις ὑμῶν ἡ πρὸς τὸν Θεόν), but nowhere
else in the N.T., though πεποίθησις πρός comes in II Cor.

iii. 4. (See an analysis of the prepositions used with πίστις in Westcott's *Hebrews* (Macmillan, 1889), on vi. 1.) If πρός is the correct reading, the variation of prepositions, πρός and εἰς, strengthens the case for restricting the object of πίστις to the Lord and of ἀγάπη to God's people. See, however, Heb. vi. 10, where love to God is virtually identified with love to God's people.

6. This is notoriously the most obscure verse in this letter.

Note, first, that ὅπως no doubt indicates the substance of the apostle's prayer (*v.* 4): '...praying that....'

But what is meant by the rest of the verse? On the whole, it seems to yield the best sense if εἰς Χριστόν is taken to mean something like 'bringing us into (closer) relation to Christ', and is connected either with ἐνεργής ('active in bringing us...') or with παντὸς ἀγαθοῦ ('every good thing that brings us...') or, possibly, with ἐπιγνώσει ('a recognition... which brings').

Dodd paraphrases: 'that the faith you hold in common with us all may work out in a clear intuition of every good thing that brings us into union with Christ.' Bultmann (in *T.W.N.T.* 1, 707f.) paraphrases: 'the faith in which Philemon participates is to become active in his recognition of what is bestowed on all the believers and what, when it comes to light, must further their connexion with Christ' (my translation).

Both these take ἡ κοινωνία τῆς πίστεώς σου as = 'the faith in which you participate', 'your share in the faith', and εἰς Χριστόν as dependent on παντὸς ἀγαθοῦ—'every good thing, or gift from God, which brings one nearer to Christ'. Others have taken it as = 'communion (with Christ) by faith'—'faith-communion with Christ'; or 'communication [to others] of your faith' (Vincent); or 'your kindly deeds of charity [communion in the sense of almsgiving], which spring from your faith' (Lightfoot); or 'your fellowship with other Christians created by faith' (Lohmeyer).

See discussions in V. Taylor, *Forgiveness and Reconciliation*
(Macmillan 1st ed., 1941), p. 132, n. 2, and George, *Communion*, p. 183.

The centre of the problem seems to lie in the interpretation of ἐν ἐπιγνώσει and εἰς Χριστόν: who is to attain to the 'recognition' or 'knowledge' in question—Philemon himself, or those who notice and profit from his 'fellowship of faith'? And in what sense is the upshot of the whole matter to be εἰς Χριστόν? On ἐπίγνωσις, see 'A Note on the Knowledge of God', p. 159. Lohmeyer draws a parallel between the function of the Law for a devout Jew, and of πίστις here for a Christian: both alike would be regarded as becoming active in the believer in finding out and doing God's will (πᾶν ἀγαθόν), with a view to the ultimate fulfilling of God's purpose for his People. But this latter sense is difficult to extract from εἰς Χριστόν.

Unless and until further ἐπίγνωσις is given to Christian interpreters, the answers to these questions must remain obscure. Meanwhile, the following three groups of quotations are intended as possible parallels to three aspects of the language:

(i) For παντὸς ἀγαθοῦ, Rom. xiv. 16 μὴ βλασφημείσθω οὖν ὑμῶν τὸ ἀγαθόν; Heb. xiii. 21 καταρτίσαι ὑμᾶς ἐν παντὶ ἀγαθῷ.... Of course, (τὸ) ἀγαθόν occurs often elsewhere, but usually as something which is *done* or *performed* (as in *v.* 14 below), rather than as a *possession* or the *object of knowledge*.

(ii) For εἰς Χριστόν, II Cor. xi. 3 μή πως...φθαρῇ τὰ νοήματα ὑμῶν ἀπὸ τῆς ἁπλότητος καὶ τῆς ἁγνότητος τῆς εἰς Χριστόν.

(iii) For the general idea that some good relationship in a Christian community between the Christians and God should become *perceptible* or *visible*, II Cor. vii. 12...ἕνεκεν τοῦ φανερωθῆναι τὴν σπουδὴν ὑμῶν τὴν ὑπὲρ ἡμῶν πρὸς ὑμᾶς ἐνώπιον τοῦ Θεοῦ.

7. ἔσχον. Probably an 'epistolary' aorist: 'I have'. See on *v.* 12 below.

τὰ σπλάγχνα τῶν ἁγίων. σπλάγχνα often means 'pity', 'sympathy' ('tender mercies')—that is, an affection directed towards others (e.g. Col. iii. 12). But in this epistle three times (see *vv.* 12, 20) it evidently means 'inmost feelings', 'very self'—that is, the recipient of the emotions rather than that which expresses them. See further on *v.* 12 below.

8–20. *The Request about Onesimus.*

8. παρρησίαν ἔχων. Of the many nuances (cf. Col. ii. 15) of this suggestive word (and its corresponding verb), which plays a distinguished part in secular literature and in Philo as well as in the N.T., the one most in place here is perhaps 'freedom to speak' authoritatively: although the apostle has perfect *liberty* to speak peremptorily, he refrains.

τὸ ἀνῆκον. See on Col. iii. 18.

9. τοιοῦτος ὤν. The participle is apparently concessive: 'although I am none other than...', yet I prefer to appeal to Christian love rather than to exercise my right to demand.

πρεσβύτης. Strictly, this meant 'an old man', whereas it was πρεσβευτής (so spelt and accented) which meant 'an ambassador'. But 'ambassador' makes excellent sense, Eph. vi. 20 is an exact parallel to the metaphor (ὑπὲρ οὗ πρεσβεύω ἐν ἁλύσει), and even if the MS. evidence indicates the 'old man' spelling, it is a negligible difference, for the two are by this time virtually interchangeable (see Preiss, *Life in Christ*, p. 176, citing Lightfoot and Lohmeyer). Translate, then, '...Paul the ambassador, yes, and now also the prisoner, of Christ Jesus'.

δέσμιος. See on *v.* 1.

10. ἐγέννησα. This metaphor of fatherhood—the evangelist 'begetting' a convert—occurs also in I Cor. iv. 15. For the metaphor of motherhood, see Gal. iv. 19. In I Pet. i. 3

God himself is spoken of as begetting Christians (cf. also I Pet. ii. 2), and in Jas. i. 18 of giving birth to them. John iii. 3–8 shows, however, that γεννάω may be used generally of procreation.

Ὀνήσιμον. The accusative—not genitive in agreement with τοῦ ἐμοῦ τέκνου—may be a mere 'attraction' with no further significance, like ὃν ἐγὼ ἀπεκεφάλισα Ἰωάννην, οὗτος ἠγέρθη, Mark vi. 16, adduced by Lightfoot. But perhaps it draws the name into close relation with ἐγέννησα: 'whom I have begotten as Onesimus'. This may be no more than a punning reference to the slave's name ('Profitable', cf. v. 20), as though to say that, at his conversion, he became true to that name for the first time. But for the more radical suggestion that 'Onesimus' was now first given him, as his 'Christian' name, see Professor J. Knox in Introduction, p. 16.

12. ἀνέπεμψα. Demonstrably an 'epistolary' aorist, to be rendered by an English present. See Col. iv. 7–9, and compare the tenses which follow below.

In its other N.T. occurrences (Luke xxiii. 7, 11, Acts xxv. 21) the verb means 'refer', in the sense of a judge sending a prisoner to some other tribunal (or 'refer back', in the case of Herod passing responsibility back to Pilate); and although (as Bauer shows) it is possible to find parallels for its use in the simple sense 'send back', it is tempting to interpret it here as a hint that St Paul wishes to 'refer Onesimus' case' to his master, rather than to send him back with the intention that he should stay for good. Cf. Professor J. Knox's use of this idea, Introduction, p. 15.

ὃν...αὐτόν. The construction may be explained as (i) a Semitic one. Hebrew has an indeclinable relative, which is followed and qualified by a direct personal pronoun, and biblical Greek sometimes imitates this (e.g. Mark vii. 25 ἧς εἶχεν τὸ θυγάτριον αὐτῆς); or (ii) an inexact but intelligible picking up of the relative by the redundant αὐτόν so as to make it natural to go on with the extension of the αὐτόν into τοῦτ' ἔστιν κ.τ.λ.: 'whom I am sending...; and when I say (I am sending) him, I mean my very self'.

σπλάγχνα. See on v. 7. Commentators at least as early as Wettstein cite evidence of σπλ. meaning 'children'. But this meaning is unlikely here, and is not attested elsewhere in the N.T. 'A part of myself' would cover most of the ideas contained in the word in the present context.

13. ἐβουλόμην is perhaps (like the aorist ἀνέπεμψα, v. 12 above) an 'epistolary' tense, to be rendered in English 'I wish' or 'I would like'. But Acts xxv. 22 shows that it could be used, without any epistolary context, in a quasi-present or conditional sense: 'I could have wished' (Lightfoot).

τοῖς δεσμοῖς τοῦ εὐαγγελίου. I.e. 'my imprisonment for the Gospel'. Cf. Phil. i. 13. Whatever were the immediate causes of imprisonment, St Paul was clear that it was ultimately due to his activity as an apostle.

15. αἰώνιον. In the context, this appears to mean 'for good', 'permanently', exactly as in Ex. xxi. 6, in the regulations for voluntary slavery, where the LXX has εἰς τὸν αἰῶνα for לְעֹלָם (cf. John viii. 35). It must not therefore be assumed (without further evidence) that αἰώνιος is here intended to carry a deeper meaning (such as it does sometimes carry) of some condition transcending time. The deeper relationship involved in common membership in the Body of Christ is described in the next verse. It is agreed by some even so that 'to get Onesimus back permanently' need not mean to receive him back as a slave so much as to acquire him permanently as a Christian brother—even if physically he is away from his master, returned to minister to Paul. (So Preiss, *Life in Christ*, and J. Knox: see Introduction, p. 15, and cf. on ἀνέπεμψα, v. 12 above.) But the τάχα γάρ, following what is said in v. 14, makes it difficult to interpret the present verse otherwise than as a reference

to the possibility of its *not* being his master's intention (γνώμη) to part with Onesimus.

16. ἀδελφὸν ἀγαπητόν. There is evidence that long before Christianity a slave who was initiated into a mystery religion was no longer reckoned as a slave, but lived with his former owner as a free man. (See Seidensticker, *Opfer*, p. 15, n. 33.) Christian initiation places the new relationship on an even deeper level. The profound implications of the word 'brother', or 'sister', in its Christian use are here hinted at. ἀδελφός, or its Semitic equivalents, was common enough even before the Christian era as a term of fellowship or comradeship, upon a racial or a religious basis: e.g., in Deut. xviii. 15 (quoted in Acts iii. 22 and elsewhere), in the common form of friendly address, Acts ii. 37, etc., and in the use of the word for devout Jews, Acts xxii. 5, xxviii. 21. But a quite new depth and intensity was given to the word by Christianity, as is indicated, e.g., by Rom. viii. 29 εἰς τὸ εἶναι αὐτὸν [i.e. Christ] πρωτότοκον ἐν πολλοῖς ἀδελφοῖς. Hence, ἀδελφός(-ή) came to be equivalent to 'a Christian', as in I Cor. v. 11 ἐάν τις ἀδελφὸς ὀνομαζόμενος..., '...if someone who is called (or calls himself?) a Christian...', ix. 4...ἀδελφὴν γυναῖκα, '...a Christian wife...' (cf. *v.* 2 above). For pagan religious use, M.M. quote a papyrus of the second century B.C., and von Soden (in *T.W.N.T. s.v.*) quotes Vettius Valens (second or third century B.C.), though this is only a vocative in address. For a discussion of the Christian use, see Harnack, *Mission and Expansion of Christianity* (English translation, 2nd ed., Williams & Norgate, 1908), I, 405 ff.

When a slave became a 'brother' to his master, there were bound to be problems, as is indicated by I Tim. vi. 2 (Christian slaves not to take liberties with Christian masters). In the present passage the matter is viewed from the other end. A brilliant portrayal of this kind of situation is to be found in Naomi Mitchison's *The Blood of the Martyrs*.

μάλιστα. In strict logic this must necessarily be used here in an 'elative' sense—'exceedingly', 'immensely'— because the following πόσῳ δὲ μᾶλλον precludes its being literally superlative. But Lightfoot prefers to treat it as an enthusiastic illogicality : 'most of all to me—*more* than most of all to thee'.

καὶ ἐν σαρκὶ καὶ ἐν Κυρίῳ. I.e. both on an ordinary, human level—as a man—and on a specifically Christian level. Not only might the unprofitable runaway now prove useful; he would also be a Christian fellow-member of the Lord's Body.

Such seems to be the sense; but it is difficult to find an exact parallel for ἐν σαρκί in this sense: κατά might rather have been the preposition expected (though II Cor. x. 3, contrasting ἐν σαρκί and κατὰ σάρκα, is not really parallel in either respect): II Cor. v. 16, οὐδένα οἴδαμεν κατὰ σάρκα, is possibly relevant, where κατὰ σάρκα goes (probably) with οἴδαμεν, to describe the manner or level of understanding.

For ἐν Κυρίῳ see on Col. i. 2, and cf. *v.* 20 below.

18. ἐλλόγα. This imperative (as though from ἐλλογάω) is rare (ἐλλογέω is the normal verb). But it is not without parallels in Hellenistic Greek, including that of the N.T.; cf. ἐλεᾷ in Rom. ix. 18 according to some MSS. (including p⁴⁶ D*); ἐλεᾶτε in Jude 22 according to some MSS.

19. ἔγραψα. An 'epistolary' aorist: see on *v.* 12 above.

For the apostle's autograph, see on Col. iv. 18.

The verse is an example of a χειρόγραφον—an autograph 'IOU', see on Col. ii. 14.

Whether the whole epistle was in St Paul's hand (as Lightfoot held) is another matter. It would be hard to prove.

ἵνα μὴ λέγω: 'not to mention that...'.

καὶ σεαυτόν κ.τ.λ. Apparently Onesimus' master owed his Christian existence—his very self—to St Paul. See Introduction, p. 20.

20. ἐγώ σου ὀναίμην. 'Let me have this benefit of you'—
the optative used in a genuinely desiderative sense: cf.
I Thess. iii. 11, v. 23, II Thess. iii. 16, II Tim. i. 18, iv. 16.
Possibly (so Lightfoot, etc.) the verb may be meant as an
allusion to Onesimus' name. The ἐγώ may, further, be
intended as emphatic (so Lightfoot, Lohmeyer): 'Let me
have this benefit—and it is to me, rather than even to
Onesimus, that it will be such.' But ἐγώ is by no means
always emphatic.

τὰ σπλάγχνα. See on *v.* 7 above. Philemon must now
prove himself true to his reputation.

ἐν Χριστῷ. See on Col. i. 2.

21–25. Personal details and farewell.

22. χαρισθήσομαι. This use of χαρίζω with a personal
object, meaning 'to grant somebody to someone', 'to hand
somebody over', is found, with a sinister connotation, in
Acts xxv. 16.

23. συναιχμάλωτος. See on Col. iv. 10.

APPENDIX OF
DISCURSIVE NOTES

APPENDIX

I. A NOTE ON CHRISTIAN GREETINGS IN LETTERS

A comparison of the greetings in Christian letters with the secular formulae of the time is instructive. Secular letters very often start with the formula 'A to B, greetings', e.g. Πολυκράτης τῶι πατρὶ χαίρειν (P. Petr. II. xi (1), third century B.C.), or '. . . (very) many greetings', πολλὰ or πλεῖστα χαίρειν; and sometimes A or B or both may be described by adjectives or designations—'A to dearest B'—and so forth. They end with 'Good luck!', εὐτύχει or εὐτυχεῖτε (e.g. P. Petr. II. xi (1), P. Par. 26), or 'Fare well!', ἔρρωσο or ἐρρῶσθαί σε εὔχομαι or (more gushing) ἐρρῶσθαί σε εὔχομαι πολλοῖς χρόνοις, κύριέ μου ἀδελφέ, or εὖ πράττετε (e.g. P. Brit. Mus. 42; pap. edited by Krebs in *Berliner Griechische Urkunden*, II, p. 174; P. Brit. Mus. 417; P. Oxy. 115). (ἔρρωσο is 2nd sing. perf. imperative pass. from ῥώννυμι, 'strengthen', and so corresponds to Latin *vale*.)

Accordingly, Acts xxiii. 26 represents Lysias' letter to Felix as beginning with Κλαύδιος Λυσίας τῷ κρατίστῳ ἡγεμόνι Φήλικι χαίρειν, though it does not include a farewell. Even the Christian encyclical letter in Acts xv. 23–9 adheres to the secular formulae χαίρειν and ἔρρωσθε (with an echo, perhaps, of the εὖ πράττετε formula in the words ἐξ ὧν διατηροῦντες ἑαυτοὺς εὖ πράξετε); and the Epistle of James has simply χαίρειν.

But the distinctively Christian formulae for beginning and end, as found in the N.T., turn the thoughts directly to God and to his generous work for man. At the head of Col., for instance, besides the Christian designation of senders and recipients, there is the formula χάρις ὑμῖν καὶ εἰρήνη ἀπὸ Θεοῦ Πατρὸς ἡμῶν. It has been ingeniously

suggested that χάρις καὶ εἰρήνη consciously combines echoes
of the ordinary Greek greeting χαίρειν and of the Semitic
shalom (cf. *salaam*), 'peace'; but it seems more likely that
the two words sprang directly from the Christian experience
of God's gracious dealings with us and the peace which is
the result (δικαιωθέντες οὖν ἐκ πίστεως εἰρήνην ἔχωμεν πρὸς
τὸν Θεόν, Rom. v. 1), and were not conscious allusions to
existing formulae. At the end of Col. comes St Paul's
autograph salutation—ὁ ἀσπασμὸς τῇ ἐμῇ χειρὶ Παύλου—and
then (after a plea to remember his imprisonment) ἡ χάρις
μεθ᾽ ὑμῶν, that is, 'God's favour is (or be) with you'.

The variations in the greetings and farewells in the N.T.
repay careful study: observe how far the non-Paulines differ
from the Paulines, in which letters ἔλεος enters the formula,
where εἰρήνη is used in the farewell, when a doxology is used,
and so forth. Further, the designations of sender(s) and re-
cipient(s) also vary significantly according to circumstances.

Here it may be noted that in I and II Thessalonians
occurs the formula τῇ ἐκκλησίᾳ Θεσσαλονικέων ἐν Θεῷ and
in Gal. i. 2 ταῖς ἐκκλησίαις τῆς Γαλατίας (ἐκκλησία thus
denoting a local 'congregation' rather than the universal
Church), whereas from the greetings in Romans and the
'Captivity Epistles' ἐκκλησία is dropped altogether; while
the Corinthian epistles have τῇ ἐκκλησίᾳ τοῦ Θεοῦ τῇ οὔσῃ
ἐν Κορίνθῳ (which could be construed to imply 'to the
universal Church as represented at Corinth'). But outside
the greetings formulae ἐκκλησία is still applied in its local
sense in Rom. xvi. 1, 4, 5, 16, I Cor. iv. 17, vii. 17, xi. 16,
xiv. 33, xvi. 1, 19, II Cor. viii. 1, 18, 19, 23, 24, xi. 8, 28,
xii. 13, and even Phil. iv. 15, Col. iv. 15, 16, Philem. 2.
It seems, therefore, that, although a universal (catholic)
conception of the Church underlies all the Epistles alike, the
word ἐκκλησία is generally used (even in the later epistles)
for a local congregation or embodiment of the Church
universal: its 'catholic' use in Eph. i. 22, iii. 10, 21, v.

passim and in Col. i. 18, 24 is exceptional. Note correspondingly that in Eph. ναός is used of the Church universal (ii. 21), whereas in I Cor. iii. 16, 17 and vi. 19 it is of a local congregation or an individual.

Finally, observe that most of the N.T. epistles are far longer than the average secular note of their day, and that their purpose and manner constitute them a new phenomenon: there had been nothing quite like the Christian epistle previously—still less, before or since, has anything quite like the Pauline epistle appeared. Further, there is a distinction to be made between the genuine *letter* and the homily in epistolary form such as some hold Hebrews and James to be. Very interesting are the observations about such matters in A. Deissmann, *Light from the Ancient East* (revised English translation from *Licht vom Osten* by L. R. M. Strachan, London, 1927), Roller, *Formular*, and P. Schubert, 'Form and Function'.

II. A NOTE ON ᾽ΑΠΟΣΤΟΛΟΣ

[See Lightfoot, *Galatians* (London, 8th ed., 1884), pp. 92 ff.; Burton, *Galatians* (Edinburgh, 1921), pp. 376 ff.; F. Jackson and K. Lake, *The Beginnings of Christianity*, vol. v (London, 1933), pp. 37 ff.; R. N. Flew, *Jesus and His Church* (Epworth Press, 1938); Knox, *Gentiles*, pp. 363 ff.; K. E. Kirk (editor), *The Apostolic Ministry* (London, 1946); J. W. Hunkin, G. Dix, H. St J. Hart in *Theology*, vol. LI (1948), pp. 166 ff., 249 ff., 341 f., 342 f.; K. Holl, *Gesammelte Aufsätze* (Tübingen, 1927–8); T. W. Manson, *The Church's Ministry* (London, 1948); V. Taylor, *St Mark* (London, 1952), pp. 619 ff.; A. Ehrhardt, *The Apostolic Succession* (Lutterworth Press, 1953); J. Munck, 'Paul, the Apostles, and the Twelve', in *Studia Theologica* (Lund) III, no. 2 (1950), pp. 96–110; D. W. B. Robinson, in *The Reformed Theological Review*, XIII, no. 2 (June 1954).]

Etymologically the word is obviously connected simply with *sending*. ᾽Απόστολος (paroxytone) means 'a naval expedition' (cf. 'mission' in its Air Force sense) in Demosthenes; and ἀπόστολος (proparoxytone) means a 'delegate' or 'messenger' or a ship sent on some errand (both in Herodotus and in the papyri). In the LXX it is very rare (only III Kingd. (=I Kings) xiv. 6 in the MS. A and in Aquila's version, and Isa. xviii. 2 in Symmachus' version). But in the N.T. it becomes very important. The following[1] is an attempt to summarize the evidence for its use and meaning in the N.T.

There are some instances where it is natural to regard the word *apostolos* as purely non-technical—meaning simply an emissary or messenger. An example is John xiii. 16 ('neither (is) one that is sent (*apostolos*) greater than he that sent him'); so, probably, are Phil. ii. 25 (Epaphroditus is the Philippians' *apostolos*) and II Cor. viii. 23 ('*apostoloi* of churches').

There are others where the term seems to be used technically, of the original 'inner circle', the Twelve. Mark iii. 14, 15 gives at least the ostensible reason for this use of the term, when, without actually calling them apostles (if we reject the longer reading), the evangelist says that Jesus appointed the twelve 'that He might send them forth (*apostello*) to preach, and to have authority to cast out devils'. Luke vi. 13, in the same connexion, says: 'whom He also named *apostoloi*'. Matt. x. 2 assumes the title *apostoloi*; and Mark himself uses it in Mark vi. 30. When Matthias was appointed to fill the gap in this body left by Judas, he was reckoned (naturally) with the Apostles; and it is possible that James the Lord's brother (who seems to be reckoned as an apostle in Gal. i. 19, and who, like Cephas and John, was called a 'pillar', Gal. ii. 9) may have been regarded as such in virtue of his filling the gap left by the martyrdom of his namesake, John's brother.[2]

[1] Reprinted, by kind permission of the Editor, from *The Office of a Bishop* (Church Book Room Press, 1948).
[2] See W. L. Knox, *St Paul and the Church of Jerusalem*, pp. 363 ff. This, however, seems unlikely: it is not death but apostasy that creates a vacancy. See C. H. Dodd, *According to the Scriptures* (London, 1952), p. 58, n. 1.

But thirdly, the term was undoubtedly also applied to a wider circle still. Whether it was so applied by persons who were conscious that they were using it in a secondary sense, or whether some people reserved the term for the Twelve while others used it more broadly, is far from certain.[1] But certain it is that in some N.T. passages others besides the Twelve are called *apostoloi*: there are Andronicus and Junias (Rom. xvi. 7, where it is most unlikely that 'of note among the apostles' only means 'well-known *to* the apostles'); there is Barnabas (Acts xiv. 14); there are *false* apostles (Rev. ii. 2, II Cor. xi. 13); and, above all, there is Paul himself. In the N.T. period we see him fighting to establish his claim to this title against detractors; but, by a strange irony, it came about that, very soon afterwards, '*the* apostle' *par excellence* meant 'Paul'.

Thus, *apostolos* appears to be a fluid term, sometimes entirely general (='emissary'), sometimes very restricted (='one of the Twelve, or of their immediate circle'), sometimes technical but broader (='a person with a special Christian commission'—cf. our 'missionary').[2] In these last two technical or semi-technical senses, can we define its characteristics? The mind naturally runs to 'Am I not an apostle? have I not seen Jesus our Lord?' (I Cor. ix. 1)—an ejaculation which suggests that an apostle proper was primarily an eyewitness. This impression is, I believe,[3] not far from the truth; but further thought both

[1] The former alternative is suggested by I Cor. xv. 1–11, II Cor. xi. 5.

[2] The word which, on the purely linguistic level, corresponds to this in Hebrew or Aramaic has been given prominence in recent discussions; but Lightfoot in *Galatians*, 8th ed. p. 93, n. 1, and E. de W. Burton in the I.C.C. commentary on Galatians years ago, and K. Lake rather more recently in *The Beginnings of Christianity*, v, pp. 48–50, seem to have said all that needs to be said about it; and it is certainly not logical to interpret the functions of a Christian *apostolos* in terms of a Jewish official merely because the terms coincide etymologically. See the articles in *Theology* cited at the head of this note.

[3] Despite the hesitation in, e.g., *The Beginnings of Christianity*, loc. cit.

modifies this and introduces other considerations besides. Paul's own claims seem[1] to be:

(a) the eyewitness function;

(b) divine commissioning to a specific task;[2]

(c) evidence of the divine confirmation of such a commission.

Now it is clear that, in Paul's case, (a) was of what might be called an irregular nature. He had not been a friend of Jesus during Jesus' ministry. He had only given allegiance to him afterwards in what we should call a supernatural and visionary meeting. So Paul's apostleship was, at any rate, not exactly like that eyewitness type which could guarantee the historical facts of the Gospel: hardly less than ourselves, Paul had to accept them on the evidence of others. There was, however, in his case the factor (b)—a direct, unmediated, divine commission (in his case, to preach to the Gentiles—see Gal. ii. 7, 8, besides other bits of evidence); and factor (c) certainly held good for him.

All three factors, then, (a), (b), and (c), belonged to the Twelve. It may well be that (b) and (c) belonged also to all apostles in the wider semi-technical sense (though (b) may, for some, have been only indirectly divine—not directly 'dominical'); but the primary question with which theories of apostolic succession are concerned is the nature of the 'greatest' apostles; and Paul's claim to be on a level with the greatest apostles seems to have rested (in his own eyes) upon the reality of (a) and (b) combined, however abnormal their manner may have been as compared with the corresponding factors in the apostleship of the Twelve: the point

---

[1] See especially I Cor. ix. 1 ff.

[2] It is highly significant that Heb. iii. 1, where *apostolos* is, strikingly, applied (together with 'High Priest') to Christ himself, corresponds to the well-attested fact that Jesus spoke of himself as 'sent' by the Father; and John xx. 21 explicitly makes the 'sending' of the disciples by Christ a parallel to the sending of Christ by the Father.

was (it would seem) that the risen Christ had himself commissioned Paul, and had specifically commissioned him to
bear witness of him (to the Gentiles, in particular).

III. A NOTE ON THE KNOWLEDGE OF GOD

[See R. P. Casey, 'The Study of Gnosticism', in *J.T.S.* xxxvi
(1935), pp. 45 ff.; R. Bultmann, *Gnosis* (trans. by J. R. Coates from
T.W.N.T.; London, 1952); E. C. Blackman, article 'Know,
Knowledge', in *A Theological Word-Book of the Bible* (ed. A.
Richardson, London: S.C.M., 1950); Dodd, *F.G.*, ch. v; J.
Dupont, *Gnosis* (Louvain, 1949), and discussions by R. Bultmann
in *J.T.S.* III (n.s.), no. 1 (April 1952) and L. Bouyer in *J.T.S.* IV
(n.s.), no. 2 (Oct. 1953); M. Dibelius in *Neutestamentliche Studien
für Heinrici* (Leipzig, 1914); K. G. Kuhn, 'Die in Palästina gefun-
denen hebräischen Texte und das N.T.' in *Z.T.K.* xlvii (1950),
pp. 192 ff.; Bo Reicke, 'Traces of Gnosticism in the Dead Sea
Scrolls?' in *J.N.T.S.* I, no. 2 (Nov. 1954); H. C. Puech, G. Quispel,
W. C. van Unnik, *The Jung Codex* (ed. F. L. Cross, London, 1955).]

There is no denying that words for knowledge often bear
special—one might say technical—meanings in religious
circles, both inside and outside Christianity. 'Christian
Science' and 'Theosophy' are modern examples of the
adaptation of such terms to a distinctively religious use.
The careful examination of these words is therefore no small
part of the study of the thought of the N.T. But it is well
to remember also that they can still be found in non-
technical senses in the N.T., and it is a mistake to assume
that they must invariably carry some abstruse inner
meaning.

(i) First, then, note that the following may reasonably
be claimed (though admittedly with varying degrees of
confidence) as quite ordinary, 'secular' uses: I Pet. iii. 7...
συνοικοῦντες κατὰ γνῶσιν ὡς ἀσθενεστέρῳ σκεύει τῷ γυναικείῳ,
ἀπονέμοντες τιμήν... (possibly = that husbands should *realize*,
κατὰ γνῶσιν, in living with their wives, that the woman
is the weaker; or, dividing the sentence differently by

putting the comma after γνῶσιν, that husbands should live with their wives *in sympathetic understanding*, rendering them honour.... See Bo Reicke in *Neutestamentliche Studien für Bultmann* (Berlin, 1954), pp. 296 ff.). This, perhaps, is the only N.T. instance of γνῶσις which might be claimed to have no clearly *theological* significance. The verb γινώσκειν, however, is frequently used for simply 'knowing' or 'perceiving': Matt. vi. 3 μὴ γνώτω ἡ ἀριστερά σου κ.τ.λ., etc.

ἐπίγνωσις seems, likewise, at least once to be used in a quite simple sense of 'recognition'—Rom. iii. 20 διὰ γὰρ νόμου ἐπίγνωσις ἁμαρτίας (it is by the Law that one recognizes what is sin); and ἐπιγινώσκειν is common enough of 'recognition', 'perception' generally: Matt. vii. 16 ἀπὸ τῶν καρπῶν αὐτῶν ἐπιγνώσεσθε αὐτούς, etc.

(ii) However, the vast preponderance of instances of these words in the N.T. is in some way *theologically* important, and, in fact, is concerned with the perception of God's will or the recognition of him in his self-revelation in Jesus Christ. Thus, the contexts in which ἐπίγνωσις usually occurs (to take only this word as an instance) speak for themselves:

Rom. i. 28. καθὼς οὐκ ἐδοκίμασαν τὸν Θεὸν ἔχειν ἐν ἐπιγνώσει,...

Rom. x. 2. ζῆλον Θεοῦ ἔχουσιν, ἀλλ' οὐ κατ' ἐπίγνωσιν.

Eph. i. 17. πνεῦμα σοφίας καὶ ἀποκαλύψεως ἐν ἐπιγνώσει αὐτοῦ.

Eph. iv. 13. εἰς τὴν ἑνότητα τῆς πίστεως καὶ τῆς ἐπιγνώσεως τοῦ Υἱοῦ τοῦ Θεοῦ.

Phil. i. 9, 10. ἵνα ἡ ἀγάπη ὑμῶν ἔτι μᾶλλον καὶ μᾶλλον περισσεύῃ ἐν ἐπιγνώσει καὶ πάσῃ αἰσθήσει, εἰς τὸ δοκιμάζειν ὑμᾶς τὰ διαφέροντα.

Col. i. 9, 10. τὴν ἐπίγνωσιν τοῦ θελήματος αὐτοῦ ἐν πάσῃ σοφίᾳ καὶ συνέσει πνευματικῇ, περιπατῆσαι ἀξίως τοῦ Κυρίου ...αὐξανόμενοι τῇ ἐπιγνώσει τοῦ Θεοῦ.

Col. ii. 2, 3. συνβιβασθέντες ἐν ἀγάπῃ καὶ εἰς πᾶν πλοῦτος τῆς πληροφορίας τῆς συνέσεως, εἰς ἐπίγνωσιν τοῦ μυστηρίου τοῦ

Θεοῦ, Χριστοῦ, ἐν ᾧ εἰσιν πάντες οἱ θησαυροὶ τῆς σοφίας καὶ γνώσεως ἀπόκρυφοι.

Col. iii. 10. τὸν νέον [ἄνθρωπον] τὸν ἀνακαινούμενον εἰς ἐπίγνωσιν κατ᾽ εἰκόνα τοῦ κτίσαντος αὐτόν, . . .

I Tim. ii. 4. πάντας . . . θέλει . . . εἰς ἐπίγνωσιν ἀληθείας ἐλθεῖν.

II Tim. ii. 25. . . . μετάνοιαν εἰς ἐπίγνωσιν ἀληθείας . . .

II Tim. iii. 7. μηδέποτε εἰς ἐπίγνωσιν ἀληθείας ἐλθεῖν δυνάμενα.

Titus i. 1. ἀπόστολος . . . κατὰ . . . ἐπίγνωσιν ἀληθείας τῆς κατ᾽ εὐσέβειαν.

Philem. 6. ἐν ἐπιγνώσει παντὸς ἀγαθοῦ τοῦ ἐν ἡμῖν εἰς Χριστόν.

Heb. x. 26. μετὰ τὸ λαβεῖν τὴν ἐπίγνωσιν τῆς ἀληθείας.

II Pet. i. 2, 3. εἰρήνη . . . ἐν ἐπιγνώσει τοῦ Θεοῦ καὶ ᾽Ιησοῦ τοῦ Κυρίου ἡμῶν . . . διὰ τῆς ἐπιγνώσεως τοῦ καλέσαντος ἡμᾶς.

II Pet. i. 8. . . . οὐκ ἀργοὺς οὐδὲ ἀκάρπους . . . εἰς τὴν τοῦ Κυρίου ἡμῶν ᾽Ιησοῦ Χριστοῦ ἐπίγνωσιν.

II Pet. ii. 20. . . . ἀποφυγόντες τὰ μιάσματα τοῦ κόσμου ἐν ἐπιγνώσει τοῦ Κυρίου καὶ Σωτῆρος ᾽Ιησοῦ Χριστοῦ. . . .

This is a complete list of all the N.T. occurrences of ἐπίγνωσις except Rom. iii. 20 (see (i) above); and it is clear that it is closely concerned with *the knowledge of Christ and conformity to his likeness*, which, in turn, is the substance of *God's self-revelation* (and this, in turn—see Bouyer, above—with the interpretation of the scriptures). Very much the same, with certain qualifications, may be said of γνῶσις.

(iii) Thus, in certain respects, N.T. usage offers an analogy to the ideas associated with what is commonly called Gnosticism—that is, a type of religious system current in the early centuries of the Christian era, which claimed to be built upon special divine knowledge or revelations.

About Gnosticism, unsubstantiated statements are too often made. Note, then:

(*a*) The term itself was not used in the ancient world as a label for this type of religion: 'Γνῶσις was used of the right apprehension of revealed truth by the orthodox and heretics alike and secondarily of a participation in the nature of God.... The word γνωστικός was used by Clement [of Alexandria] to characterize the Christian philosopher and was assumed as a title by the Ophites [a heretical sect].... There is no trace in early Christianity of "Gnosticism" as a broad historical category...' (Casey, as above).

(b) On the other hand, there evidently did exist a large though ill-defined religious movement, to which this title of Gnosticism has come to be applied. Our existing documentary evidence for such a movement cannot be securely dated earlier than Christianity, although the newly discovered Dead Sea Scrolls show some affinities with it (see Kuhn, and, for qualifications regarding their use of *yada'*, 'to know', Bo Reicke, as above). But we can profitably ask whether its main features do not help to explain some of the conflict lying behind Colossians and other N.T. writings. 'Gnosticism' (to use the term, however anachronistically) showed two main features: first, a radical 'dualism', as between the visible world (with the spirit-powers which were believed to stand behind it), and a higher world, unknown to most men, whence comes the soul (at least of those destined for salvation). Secondly, there was the idea that the true 'gnostic' could be rescued from this visible, evil world into that other higher world of truth by secret knowledge, 'gnosis'.

(iv) How much the Christian vocabulary owes to pagan thought is disputed. Dupont (as above) is disposed to trace it rather to Judaism. But it is conceivable, and in some cases likely, that Christian writers spoke of their own γνῶσις in conscious allusion to this gnostic type of religion.

But if so, it was in conscious distinction from it; for if it shared with 'Gnostic' systems the idea that salvation came by truth divinely revealed, that was where the likeness ended. The Christian γνῶσις was not confined to an inner circle of élite initiates: every Christian, as such, possessed it; and the Christian γνῶσις was not the knowledge merely of certain propositions about the nature of God—still less of the pass-words which might be hoped to admit the initiate to heaven: it was a *relationship* with a *personal* God who had revealed himself *in Jesus Christ*. Just as in the O.T. 'to know God' meant far more than to know *about* God—it meant obedience and a response of the will; and just as the God of the O.T. was revealed in his great *actions* in history, and not merely by statements communicated through theologians: so, still more, Christian γνῶσις meant a response of the whole person—will as well as mind—to God as revealed in *the* supreme historical event, the ministry, death, and resurrection of Jesus.[1]

(v) It is true that a passage like I Cor. viii. 10, 11 might (if viewed alone) suggest that St Paul recognized γνῶσις as something not shared in common by all Christians; but other passages suggest that, if there was any *exclusive* meaning attaching to truly Christian γνῶσις, it was one which excluded non-Christians but included all Christians alike: I Cor. xv. 34, II Cor. ii. 14. Similarly Christian σοφία is distinguished sharply from all merely worldly wisdom or philosophy; but within the Christian Church it stands for the Gospel which was common to all alike (I Cor. i. 24). An excellent analogy is provided also by the N.T. use of μυστήριον, on which see the notes on Col. i. 26. Regarding all these words, and many others besides, the truly distinctive feature of the N.T. usage is that they can be virtually equated with Christ himself: he *is* (or *includes*) γνῶσις (Col. ii. 3), τὸ μυστήριον (Col. ii. 2), σοφία (I Cor. i. 24, Col. ii. 3), δόξα (II Cor. iv. 6, Heb. i. 3, Jas. ii. 1), and ἀλήθεια (John xiv. 6, Eph. iv. 21 (?)). 'Christianity is Christ.' As always, the distinctive quality in the Christian faith lies in its estimate of Jesus of Nazareth, who suffered under

[1] For early 'Gnosis', see now *The Jung Codex, ut supra.*

Pontius Pilate, as in a unique sense divine: hence, all the words for divine revelation converge upon him, and all apprehension of divine revelation becomes a matter of personal relationship, not only of intellectual assent.

See also the remarks on Col. i. 9.

IV. A NOTE ON ΠΛΗΡΩΜΑ

There are two classic dissertations in English on the meaning of πλήρωμα, by Lightfoot on Colossians and by Armitage Robinson, *Eph.* Armitage Robinson (partly in contradiction to Lightfoot's findings) made a good case against πλήρωμα meaning 'that which is filled'. (Delling, in *T.W.N.T. s.v.*, discusses this meaning, among the others. But Hesychius and Stephanus do not seem to bear it out; and even the following from Philo are not, I believe, conclusive: *de Praem. et Poen.* 65; 109; *de Spec. Legg.* I, 272; *Quod Omnis Prob.* 41.) Rather, πλήρωμα means 'that which fills or completes' or 'the (resulting) completeness'. This covers most of the biblical uses, in O.T. and N.T.; e.g. 'the earth and *all that therein is*', Ps. xxiv (LXX xxiii). 1, I Cor. x. 26, etc., the *patch*, filling a hole in a torn garment, Matt. ix. 16, the food which *filled* the baskets, Mark viii. 20, the *total* of Gentiles destined to be brought into the Church (or, possibly, all the Gentiles that there are), Rom. xi. 25. Similarly Lucian is cited as referring to the fighting of a naval battle with so many πληρώματα, i.e. 'full crews', 'ships fully manned' (cf. the modern use of 'strength', 'establishment', 'full complement', in reference to a fully manned company or staff). Many also adduce for this sense Rom. xiii. 10, where ἀγάπη is the πλήρωμα of the Law, as though this meant that ἀγάπη was the *sum total* of all the injunctions of the Law. But here it is possible that πλήρωμα means 'fulfilment': to love is to establish, to complete, to bring to realization all that the Law intends (cf. Gal. vi. 2).

It is true that strictly the termination -μα indicates something *concrete* ('that which fills'), and that *fulfilment* (abstract) should be πλήρωσις. But the line between the two is thin: see Rom. v. 16, 18 where δικαίωμα seems = δικαίωσις; and, conversely, Ezek. xxxii. 15 (LXX) where πλήρωσις = πλήρωμα.

Beginning, now, the examination of the Colossians use from Col. i. 19, in that passage the choice seems to lie between interpreting πᾶν τὸ πλήρωμα as 'the entirety [of God's attributes]', 'full divinity', or as a technical term of 'Gnostic' thought, signifying 'all the supernatural denizens of the interspace between the invisible, uncreated God and the visible, created world'.

In favour of the latter the following considerations may be advanced:

(i) Although it is not correct to speak of 'Gnosticism' as though it were a clearly defined creed (at least not as early as St Paul—see A Note on the Knowledge of God, p. 161, (iii)), yet it is true that any dualistic system is prone to imagine a kind of bridge or chain of beings representing the transition from the pure immateriality of God to the evil world of matter (the very terms are dualistic, not Christian), a sort of descending scale growing progressively more material, less divine, more remote from perfection; and it is known that the Valentinians[1] (a 'Gnostic' sect of the second century) and possibly the Cerinthians, a little earlier (see Lightfoot, pp. 264–6), used the term πλήρωμα to describe the region inhabited by the 'sum total', 'the full strength' of this contingent of intermediary beings—'a harmonious society or hierarchy of spiritual essences' (Dodd, *F.G.*, p. 105). Therefore,

[1] Though apparently Valentinus himself, to judge by *The Jung Codex* (see bibliography in A Note on the Knowledge of God, p. 159), pp. 53, 98, did not hold the beliefs about this hierarchy of beings which were attributed to his followers. For πλήρωμα and ὑστέρημα in the Jung Codex, see *op. cit.* pp. 47, 94, 96.

(ii) if we may assume that the false teachers at Colossae believed Christ to be only one member of such a hierarchy (and not necessarily a high-ranking one), and if we may assume that it was already collectively styled πᾶν τὸ πλήρωμα, then there is much force in the apostle's assertion that, on the contrary, in Christ resides 'the *total*': whatever 'powers' there may be are collectively included in him.

This is plausible and suggestive, especially when πλήρωμα is, as here, used absolutely (contrast ii. 9); but, although it is very possible that St Paul's vocabulary included technical terms borrowed from the 'Gnostic' armoury, evidence is lacking that the technical use of πλήρωμα was ever wide-spread—least of all as early as this.

In favour of the alternative interpretation as 'the entirety, the sum total, of the divine attributes' (a more general, less technical, sense) are the following considerations:

(i) In ii. 9 the phrase is specifically πᾶν τὸ πλήρωμα τῆς Θεότητος, and ἡ Θεότης cannot possibly be equated with the Gnostics' hierarchy of beings lying between God and the world: it must mean 'deity', 'Godhead'.

(ii) The phrase in ii. 3, ἐν ᾧ εἰσιν πάντες οἱ θησαυροὶ τῆς σοφίας καὶ γνώσεως ἀπόκρυφοι, supports this interpretation: Christ is or contains the entirety of the divine Wisdom.

(iii) πλήρωμα was so common a word in the Greek O.T.[1] that one would need strong evidence to drive one to look to an external source for its primary meaning in a writer so steeped in his O.T. as St Paul.

(iv) The other occurrences of πλήρωμα in the N.T. are none of them such as to compel one to interpret them in a technical sense; the nearest to the use under discussion is—apart from the use in Ephesians, which will be considered

---

[1] And note its use in the *Corpus Hermeticum*: πλ. τῆς ζωῆς applied to the world, XII. 15; πλ. τῆς κακίας applied to the world, and πλ. τοῦ ἀγαθοῦ to God in VI. 4 (Dodd, *F.G.*, pp. 18, 21).

directly—perhaps in John i. 16 ἐκ τοῦ πληρώματος αὐτοῦ ἡμεῖς πάντες ἐλάβομεν; and this, in its turn, is perhaps illuminated by John iii. 34 ὃν γὰρ ἀπέστειλεν ὁ Θεὸς τὰ ῥήματα τοῦ Θεοῦ λαλεῖ· οὐ γὰρ ἐκ μέτρου δίδωσιν τὸ Πνεῦμα: in other words, πλήρωμα is used to convey much the same idea as the 'Logos doctrine' which sees in Christ the full and comprehensive message of God embodied, in contrast to the partial and fragmentary quality of any other sort of inspiration (cf. the opening words of Hebrews). Perhaps something very similar, in even more general terms, may be intended by the words, in Rom. viii. 32... σὺν αὐτῷ τὰ πάντα ἡμῖν χαρίσεται—in giving us Christ, God gives us all, he gives us his πλήρωμα. Cf. also the famous saying in Matt. xi. 27, Luke x. 22.

(v) The use of πλήρωμα in Ephesians calls for special notice. It brings to light a further idea which seems to be relevant also in Colossians—namely, that in some sense πλήρωμα may be applied to the Church as well as to Christ; but it does not lend support to a technical, 'Gnostic' sense. The occurrences in Ephesians are as follows:

i. 10. εἰς οἰκονομίαν τοῦ πληρώματος τῶν καιρῶν, i.e. (probably) 'to be dispensed when the opportunity was fully ripe' (a normal and not essentially theological use of πλ., as = 'full amount'), although it may carry the additional association of God's predetermined plan being completed (cf. Delling, in T.W.N.T., s.v.).

i. 22, 23. ...καὶ αὐτὸν ἔδωκεν κεφαλὴν ὑπὲρ πάντα τῇ ἐκκλησίᾳ, ἥτις ἐστὶν τὸ σῶμα αὐτοῦ, τὸ πλήρωμα τοῦ τὰ πάντα ἐν πᾶσιν πληρουμένου. This is notoriously problematic. Four main types of interpretation emerge:

(a) Taking πληρουμένου as passive, the Church is to be the *completion* (πλήρωμα) of Christ who will (as the Church grows) be totally (τὰ πάντα ἐν πᾶσιν) *completed*. (An alternative interpretation within this type is that Christ is to be completed by the Church as the head is completed by the body: but this, however well supported by later 'Gnostic' parallels, is surely too naïve, and less compatible with the N.T. conception of Christ than the more general idea of the Church as his fulfilment.)

(b) Taking πληρουμένου as middle with an active sense, the Church is the *completion* of Christ who is totally (ἐν πᾶσιν) filling (πληρουμένου) everything (τὰ πάντα) (or, filling absolutely everything—τὰ πάντα ἐν πᾶσιν). So A.V. and R.V. (apparently).

(c) Taking πληρουμένου again as active, but πλήρωμα as a 'passive noun', the Church is *that which is filled* (πλήρωμα) by the all-filling Christ. But this appears to be contrary to the evidence for the meaning of πλήρωμα (see Robinson, *Eph.*, cited above).

(d) Once more, taking πληρουμένου as active in sense, and taking τὸ πλήρωμα as in apposition to αὐτόν (Christ) instead of to ἡ ἐκκλησία, Christ has been appointed by God to be not only supreme head to the Church but also the fulness— the all-inclusive representative—of God the all-filler.[1]

This was defended by A. E. N. Hitchcock in *E.T.* XXII (1910–11), p. 91, and by me in *E.T.* LX (1948–9), pp. 53, 224, though Abbott *in loc.* calls it impossible Greek, and Best, *One Body*, p. 144, n. 1, 'grammatically difficult'. It has the advantage of bringing τὸ πλήρωμα into line with the Colossians passages, and it fits exactly with the thought of I Cor. xv. 28 where God is ultimately to be πάντα ἐν πᾶσιν, and of Eph. iv. 10 where Christ's death and resurrection are seen to have as result ἵνα πληρώσῃ τὰ πάντα: i.e. Christ represents the all-pervasiveness of God.

Against all the interpretations (b)–(d) is the fact that πληροῦσθαι appears not to occur elsewhere with an active sense; but against (a) is the consistent representation else-

---

[1] Cf. Jer. xxiii. 24 ...μὴ οὐχὶ τὸν οὐρανὸν καὶ τὴν γῆν ἐγὼ πληρῶ; λέγει Κύριος, and *Corpus Hermeticum* XI. 5 ἅπαντα γὰρ πλήρη τοῦ θεοῦ (Dodd, *F.G.* p. 20).

where of Christ as actively *filling*, not as passively *being filled* (even if τὰ ὑστερήματα τῶν θλίψεων τοῦ Χριστοῦ may be said to be filled up, Col. i. 24, and even if the Body of Christ is yet to be built up, Eph. iv. 12). The remaining two Ephesians passages are—

iii. 19. ἵνα πληρωθῆτε εἰς πᾶν τὸ πλήρωμα τοῦ Θεοῦ, and

iv. 12, 13. . . . εἰς οἰκοδομὴν τοῦ σώματος τοῦ Χριστοῦ, μέχρι καταντήσωμεν οἱ πάντες εἰς τὴν ἑνότητα τῆς πίστεως καὶ τῆς ἐπιγνώσεως τοῦ Υἱοῦ τοῦ Θεοῦ, εἰς ἄνδρα τέλειον, εἰς μέτρον ἡλικίας τοῦ πληρώματος τοῦ Χριστοῦ,. . .

In both of these, τὸ πλήρωμα (of God or of Christ) is the condition, astonishingly, to which Christians are destined to be brought: they are to be 'filled up to the full maturity intended by God' (if that is what iii. 19 means), they are to 'attain to the full growth of manhood, the standard (μέτρον) consisting in the full stature (ἡλικίας) of the full maturity belonging to Christ'(?). Cf. John xvii. 23 ἵνα ὦσιν τετελειωμένοι εἰς ἕν ('brought to a complete unity'), Col. ii. 10 ἐστὲ ἐν αὐτῷ πεπληρωμένοι.

Putting all these clues together, it appears that Christ is thought of as containing, representing, all that God is; and that the destiny of Christians, as the Body of Christ, is to enter, in him, into that wealth and completeness. This holds good even if one suspends judgment over the difficult Eph. i. 22, 23; and it is strikingly illustrated by the astonishing claims of I Cor. iii. 21-23 (everything belongs to you, because you belong to Christ).

V. A NOTE ON THE REFLEXIVE PRONOUN

Supposing that Christ *were*, after all, taken as subject of εὐδόκησεν in Col. i. 19, then ἐν αὐτῷ and δι' αὐτοῦ would require to bear a reflexive sense—'in himself', etc. In any case, the εἰς αὐτόν must do so. Note, then:

(i) It is well known that ἑαυτόν was sometimes contracted

to αὐτόν, though the contraction was becoming less frequent in the Hellenistic period than it had been formerly (D.-B., § 64. 1, *Anh.*).

(ii) In the older MSS. breathings and accents are omitted, and an editor is therefore free to choose, except when a preceding word such as οὐκ, οὐχ shows which is intended (see W.H. ii. 144b).

(iii) Therefore one is entitled to interpret αυτον etc. according to context, and there are certainly some N.T. passages which call for a reflexive interpretation: Luke xxiii. 12 ἐν ἔχθρᾳ ὄντες πρὸς αυτους (evidently = ἑαυτούς = ἀλλήλους), xxiv. 12 ἀπῆλθεν πρὸς αυτον, John xiii. 32 ὁ Θεὸς δοξάσει αυτον ἐν αυτῳ (i.e. ? αὐτὸν ἐν αὑτῷ), Eph. i. 5 προορίσας ἡμᾶς εἰς υἱοθεσίαν διὰ Ἰησοῦ Χριστοῦ εἰς αυτον, ii. 15 ἵνα τοὺς δύο κτίσῃ ἐν αυτῳ..., Rev. xviii. 7 ὅσα ἐδόξασεν αυτην.... (In most of these passages there are variant readings with the uncontracted reflexive forms, cf. I John v. 18.)

(iv) However, D.-B. (*loc. cit.*) regards the genitive form αὐτοῦ as scarcely extant in Hellenistic Greek (W.H. retain it in Matt. vi. 34, II Cor. iii. 5. Note, too, that the contracted dative is found: see John xiii. 32, Eph. ii. 15 above, and Luke xii. 21). This tells against taking Christ as the subject of εὐδόκησεν (for δι' αυτου would then need to be taken reflexively).

(v) Lightfoot (*in loc.*) maintains that the use of the non-reflexive forms αὐτόν etc. in a reflexive sense was becoming common, and he prints αὐτόν here but interprets reflexively (with 'the Father' as subject).

If God, or πᾶν τὸ πλήρωμα, is taken as the subject, then it will be clearest to print: ὅτι ἐν αὐτῷ εὐδόκησεν πᾶν τὸ πλήρωμα κατοικῆσαι καὶ δι' αὐτοῦ ἀποκαταλλάξαι τὰ πάντα εἰς αὐτόν,...